SPARKNOTES™

101

Political Science

D0188220

SPARK PUBLISHING

SPARKNOTES is a registered trademark of SparkNotes LLC

Spark Publishing
A Division of Barnes & Noble
120 Fifth Avenue
New York, NY 10011
www.sparknotes.com

ISBN-13: 978-1-4114-9855-6
ISBN-10: 1-4114-9855-0

Please submit all comments and questions or report errors to www.sparknotes.com/errors.

Library of Congress Cataloging-in-Publication Data available upon request.

Printed and bound in the United States.

10 9 8 7 6 5 4 3 2 1

Contents

Chapter 5

Chapter 6

Acknowledgments

SparkNotes would like to thank the following writers and contributors:

Paul Glenn, PhD in Political Science

Joshua Cracraft, Graduate Student, American History
Brandeis University

Andrew J. Waskey, MA in Theology
Professor, Division of Social Sciences
Dalton State College

John W. Sutherlin, PhD in International Relations
Assistant Professor, Department of History and Government
University of Louisiana at Monroe

A Note from SparkNotes

Welcome to the *SparkNotes 101* series! This book will help you succeed in your introductory college course for political science.

Every component of this study guide has been designed to help you process the material more quickly and score higher on your exams. You'll see lots of headings, lists, and charts, and, most important, you won't see any long blocks of text. This format will allow you to quickly learn what you need to know.

We've included these features to help you get the most out of this book:

Introduction: Before diving into the major chapters, you may want to get a broader view of the field of political science. The Introduction discusses the development of political science as an academic field; introduces some major thinkers and figures; lists the important subfields of political science, including American politics; explains the relationship between political science and the other social sciences; and describes some possible career paths for students interested in pursuing further study.

Chapters 1–6: Each chapter provides clarification of material included in your textbook as well as the following:

- **Shaded Text Boxes:** These call out main points and provide related information.

- **Examples:** These clarify main points and show you how concepts from political science work throughout the world.

- **Key Terms:** Important terms are bolded throughout each chapter for quick review. Definitions for these terms are compiled in the glossary at the back of the book.

- **Sample Test Questions:** The study questions, including true/false, multiple choice, and short answer, show you the kinds of questions you're most likely to encounter on a test and give you the chance to practice what you've learned. Answers are provided.

- **Suggested Reading:** This list makes recommendations for enhancing your knowledge with further research in notable books.

- **Useful Websites:** This list shows you where to go on the web to get more information or explore a topic in depth.

A+ Student Essays: These are the real thing. These essays show you how to pull together the facts and concepts you've learned in your course to make a compelling argument. They also show you the kinds of concerns scholars grapple with. We should point out that the essays do not reflect the political opinions of the writers or contributors of this book, SparkNotes, or the publishers.

Glossary: Review new terms and refresh your memory at exam time.

Index: Turn to the index at the back of the book to look up specific concepts, terms, and people.

Your textbook might be longer or look different than our study guide. Not to worry—we've got you covered. Everything you need is here. We've gone for concision to make your studying easier. The material is organized in a clear, logical way that won't overwhelm you—but will give you everything you need to know to keep up in class.

We hope *SparkNotes 101: Political Science* helps you, gives you confidence, and occasionally saves your butt! Your input makes us better. Let us know what you think or how we can improve this book at **www.sparknotes.com/comments.**

Introduction

Political science is the systematic study of government and power. Political scientists examine a wide range of topics, from how laws get made to why wars are fought to how political parties develop and win elections. Because power takes many forms, political science often overlaps with economics, psychology, sociology, and the other social sciences.

The Development of Political Science

For as long as humans have formed communities, people have debated and analyzed **politics,** or the way groups of people, particularly governments, reach agreements and make decisions that will affect the entire society.

THE ANCIENT AND MEDIEVAL WORLDS

The word *politics* comes from the Greek word *polis,* which means "city-state." Probably the first person to use the term *political science* was Aristotle, a Greek philosopher who argued in favor of living a virtuous life.

Political science in the ancient and medieval worlds was closely linked to philosophy and theology. It often consisted of advice for rulers on how to govern justly. Numerous thinkers and scholars advanced the study of politics and government, including:

- **Plato (c. 427–c. 347 BCE):** One of the greatest western philosophers, Plato wrote several dialogues about political matters, including *The Republic* (c. 360 BCE).

- **Aristotle (384–322 BCE):** A student of Plato's, Aristotle applied empirical methods to the study of politics.

- **St. Augustine (CE 354–430):** Augustine's *City of God* (419) argued for the centrality of salvation to life, even with regard to politics.

- **St. Thomas Aquinas (1225–1274):** Aquinas helped re-introduce Aristotle to Europe and melded Aristotelian thought with Christianity.

MODERN EUROPE

In the fifteenth century, Europe began to change dramatically as the modern world slowly emerged. In art, science, economics, religion, and politics, Europeans started to break away from tradition and forge new ways of understanding the world. Among the key thinkers of this time were political philosophers, who attempted to establish a systematic understanding of politics. These thinkers include:

- **Niccolo Machiavelli (1469–1527):** Machiavelli's book *The Prince* (written c. 1513; published in 1532) portrayed politics as a struggle for power, and in it he urged rulers to lie, cheat, and kill to get ahead.

- **Thomas Hobbes (1588–1679):** Hobbes attempted to use the methods of geometry to arrive at an irrefutable science of politics. Hobbes argued for absolute monarchy.

- **John Locke (1632–1704):** Locke argued for a democratic government that respected individual and property rights. His writings greatly influenced Thomas Jefferson, as reflected in the Declaration of Independence.

- **Jean-Jacques Rousseau (1712–1778):** Rousseau's iconoclastic attack on tradition contributed to the French Revolution. His book *The Social Contract* (1762) states, "Man is born free, and he is everywhere in chains," an important sentiment during the American and French revolutions.

INDUSTRIALIZATION AND EMPIRE

As the Industrial Revolution overtook Europe and the United States in the nineteenth century, social theorists began to change their approach to political science. They began relying on statistical data and empirical observation to understand politics; in this way, these thinkers began to emphasize the science part of political science. Universities also began creating political science departments, which cemented the status of political science as an academic discipline. Some significant philosophers and thinkers from this period include:

- **Karl Marx (1818–1883):** A philosopher and social scientist who saw the economy as the key institution in society. He argued that employers in a capitalist society exploit their workers and that the capitalist classes pass laws to benefit themselves. His books *The Communist Manifesto* and *Capital* spurred the Russian Revolution of 1917.

- **John William Burgess (1844–1931):** A professor who created a political science department at Columbia University that sought to train students for a life of public service. This was the first such department in the United States, and it helped institutionalize and legitimize political science as an academic discipline.

- **Herbert Baxter Adams (1850–1901):** A professor who introduced seminar-style learning into colleges in the United States. According to legend, Adams was the first westerner to use the term *political science* (Aristotle was the first person to use the term itself).

- **Max Weber (1864–1920):** An economist and sociologist who argued that religion, not economics, is the central force in social change. According to Weber, Protestants seeking an outward affirmation of their godliness brought about the birth of capitalism.

THE TWENTIETH CENTURY AND BEYOND

In the 1950s, a new approach to political science called **behavioralism** emerged. Behavioralists argued that political scientists should focus on behavior, not institutions or motives. Although behavioralism has been heavily debated, it remains the predominant paradigm in political science today. Some of the most influential contemporary political scientists include:

- **Gabriel Almond (1910–2002):** A professor who not only developed the concept of political culture but also revolutionized the subfield of comparative politics. *The Politics of the Developing Areas* (1960), which he co-authored, opened the doors for American political scientists to begin studying the political processes at work in non-Western countries.

- **David Easton (1917–):** The professor who developed the behavioral model of political science in the 1950s. *The Political System: An Inquiry into the State of Political Science* (1953) is probably his most famous work.

- **John Rawls (1921–2002):** A professor who was widely considered to be the most important political philosopher of the twentieth century. His book *A Theory of Justice* (1971) argued that we should strive to develop a society based on equality.

- **Robert O. Keohane (1941–):** A professor who helped develop the neoliberal theory of international relations. A 2005 poll in the journal *Foreign Policy* named him the most influential scholar of international relations.

Fields of Study

The overall field of political science includes several major subfields: American government, comparative politics, international relations, political economy, and political philosophy. Most political science departments at universities encourage students to specialize or concentrate in one of these subfields.

AMERICAN GOVERNMENT

The biggest subfield of political science in the United States, American government focuses on voting behavior, political parties, lawmaking, the Constitution, public administration, public policy, the role of the courts, and other facets of American government. Some departments refer to this subfield as "civics."

COMPARATIVE POLITICS

Comparative politics compares systems of government in other countries. For example, a comparative political scientist might examine the impact of political parties on elections in Australia, the United Kingdom, and the United States, or she might compare the constitutions of Argentina and Barbados.

INTERNATIONAL RELATIONS

International relations scholars examine the ways in which nations interact. Whereas comparative politics *compare* the internal workings of a state, international relations focuses on how states *relate* to one another, such as why and how states trade, cooperate, and fight.

POLITICAL ECONOMY

Political economy is the study of how economics and politics affect each other. Political scientists in this subfield might look at the impact of economic power on international relations or how different economies develop within similar political systems.

POLITICAL PHILOSOPHY

Some political scientists study the tradition of political philosophies from Plato to the present. This subfield tries to answer questions and develop theories about such abstract issues as ethics, authority, the nature of liberty and freedom, the meaning of civil rights and civil liberties, and how governments should function.

The Other Social Sciences

Social sciences study how people interact with and relate to one another. Political science, with its emphasis on political systems and the distribution of power, falls into this larger academic category. A multidisciplinary field, political science draws from some other social sciences, including sociology, economics, psychology, and anthropology.

SOCIOLOGY

Sociology studies social life and human interactions, from how groups form to how large organizations run to how people interact with one another. Political scientists make use of sociological studies and methods when examining, for example, how small group dynamics affect the decision-making process, how people acquire and maintain power, and how political culture shapes our attitudes.

ECONOMICS

Politics and economics often intersect. Studying government without also studying economics, especially in free-market societies such as the United States, is not possible. Political scientists examine such economic issues as the effects government policy has on the economy, the role money plays in campaigns, and how nations arrive at trade agreements.

PSYCHOLOGY

Psychology studies the way the human mind works, helping us to understand why people behave the way that they do. Political scientists sometimes use the insights of psychology to analyze a president's or voter's behavior or to explain why some people are more prone to supporting certain governments and ideologies.

ANTHROPOLOGY

Anthropology examines cultures within a society and theorizes about how those cultures affect society. Anthropologists explore how people acquire cultural values. Because culture often has a strong effect on behavior, political scientists rely on anthropological studies and methods.

What Political Scientists Do

Politics and government affect almost every element of our lives, so it makes sense that a political science background is useful in many different fields.

PUBLIC POLICY

Government policy affects nearly everything that we do, so public policy experts can work in a variety of areas:

- Issue advocate
- Government official
- Activist
- City planner
- Legislative analyst

CAMPAIGNS

Many political science majors spend time working on campaigns, which can lead to one of several careers in politics:

- Pollster
- Event organizer
- Public opinion analyst
- Communications director

LAW AND LAW ENFORCEMENT

Many students of political science go on to choose one of the following careers in law and law enforcement:

- Attorney
- Judge
- Police officer
- Parole officer
- FBI or CIA agent
- Prison administrator

BUSINESS

Although political science does not deal directly with business matters, it does teach the analytical and data interpretation skills needed for many careers in the private sector. Political scientists interested in working in business might take the following kinds of jobs:

- Bank executive
- Career counselor
- Corporate economist
- Government relations manager
- Management analyst
- Systems analyst

EDUCATION

Many political scientists earn a PhD and do specialized research and scholarship at a "think tank." Still others may choose one of the following jobs:

- Professor
- High school teacher
- Educational curriculum developer
- Journal editor

This list covers just a few of the careers open to students of political science majors. As you will see in your studies of political science, the discipline teaches many skills, including critical thinking and analytical reasoning, which can be applied in many fields.

POLITICS AND POLITICAL SCIENCE

1

Overview

Politics impact our lives every day. Our political choices determine our government, which, in turn, determines whether we can vote or consume alcohol, how much we pay in taxes, whether we can serve in the armed forces, which utilities we use, where we can build a home, whether we can run a business in that home, how much money we can get as a loan for educational expenses, and even which types of food we eat. Just about everything in our lives is affected by politics and government.

The democratic system of government in the United States is just one way of organizing a political system. Throughout history, there have been many systems of government and many different types of democracies. Political science is the attempt to study politics and government in a systematic way in order to learn how power works. Political scientists study systems of government and democracies, as well as how governments relate to one another and how political systems change over time. As an academic discipline, political science is fairly new, but people have studied politics for thousands of years.

What Is Political Science?

Political science is the systematic study of **politics,** or the process by which governmental decisions are made. As a famous definition puts it, politics is determining who gets what, where, when, and how. The political scientist is an objective observer who asks questions about and studies the effects and structures of different systems of governments.

A BRIEF HISTORY OF POLITICAL SCIENCE

Political science originated with the ancient Greeks in the first century BCE. During this time, the philosopher Plato wrote numerous dialogues about politics, asking about the nature of justice, what constitutes good government, and what is truly best for humanity. His student Aristotle worked in a more scientific way, observing and describing types of governments systematically. At the start of the seventeenth century, people began to apply the methods of the scientific revolution to politics. Thomas Hobbes, for example, employed the methods of geometry to break government down into its most basic parts in order to understand it. In the nineteenth century, thinkers such as Karl Marx and Max Weber used sociological methods to analyze politics.

POLITICAL SCIENCE TODAY

In the last few decades, political science has become more solidly established. Political professionals work on campaigns (as well as news shows) at all levels to help sway voters, and many elected officials analyze data to help make policy choices. Today, many political scientists use statistics and other quantitative methods to study a variety of issues, such as voting, Congress, and the presidency.

Key Terms

Political scientists rely on several important concepts:

- **Power:** The ability to get others to do what you want. Power can take many forms, from brute force to articulate persuasion.

- **Government:** The organization of power within a society, specifically how power is divided and used.

  EXAMPLE: The government of the United States is a democracy established by the Constitution.

- **Regime:** Any particular government.

- **Legitimacy:** Occurs when citizens accept the political decisions made by the governing body. A government is considered **legitimate** if its citizens think it right, lawful, and proper that the government should hold power. A threat to legitimacy seriously undermines the power of the government.

- **Authority:** The ability of the government to exercise power without resorting to violence. A government with a high level of legitimacy tends to have a high level of authority. Its citizens usually obey the law because they think it is the right thing to do, not because they are afraid of punishment.

    EXAMPLE: When asked by a police officer to clear the street, most Americans will do so because they respect the right of the officer to use power.

- **Sovereignty:** The right to exercise political power over a group of people or a geographical area. A government is considered **sovereign** if it has the final word on political decisions within its boundaries. When citizens can appeal to a higher body, the government is not sovereign.

    EXAMPLE: State governments in the United States have a great deal of power, but ultimately they are not sovereign because the federal government can overrule them.

Types of Regimes

Political scientists refer to regimes using many different terms. Which term political scientists use often depends on two factors: the number of people with political power and the amount of power the government itself exerts.

The chart below organizes regimes by the number of people who hold political power.

REGIMES AND NUMBER OF PEOPLE WITH POWER		
Type of Regime	**Number of People Who Hold Power**	**Example**
Monarchy	One	Nepal, Saudi Arabia, Jordan, Brunei, medieval England
Dictatorship	One	Libya, Cuba, North Korea, Nazi Germany
Aristocracy	A few (usually a small ruling class)	Ancient Sparta
Oligarchy	A few (usually a small group of wealthy individuals)	Renaissance Venice
Democracy	Many or all	United States, ancient Athens

A wide variety of regime types exist. For example, the United Kingdom has a constitutional monarchy, in which Queen Elizabeth holds a limited amount of power. Theoretically, the queen is the English head of state, but over time the English monarchy has become largely ceremonial. Real governmental power now rests with the Parliament, the legislative, lawmaking body. In contrast, the Third Reich of World War II was a totalitarian dictatorship. Adolf Hitler controlled the government and the citizens of Nazi Germany.

The chart on the next page organizes regimes by the amount of power the government possesses.

CHAPTER 1

REGIMES AND AMOUNT OF GOVERNMENT POWER		
Type of Regime	Amount of Governmental Power	Example
Totalitarian	Absolute power; controls every aspect of its citizens' lives	Soviet Union, North Korea, Nazi Germany
Autocratic	Less powerful than a totalitarian regime but still controls most aspects of its citizens' lives; often associated with a single ruler; often arbitrary	Iraq before the 2003 American invasion
Authoritarian	Less power than totalitarian regime but still controls most aspects of its citizens' lives; often outlasts its rulers	China, Egypt
Constitutional	Limited by specific rules, such as the citizens' right to free speech or freedom of religion	United States, United Kingdom, Germany, Japan
Anarchist	No power, or simply no government; can occur when a government loses its power	Somalia

DEMOCRACIES

The word *democracy* comes from the Greek words *demos*, which means "the people," and *cracy*, which means "rule by." Today, we call a regime a **democracy** when many or all of its people share political power. There are two types of democracies:

• **Direct democracy:** Citizens make all the decisions. They gather frequently to vote on laws, regulations, and appointments. There are no elected representatives. Direct democracy was common in ancient Greece; today, it exists at a local level in town hall meetings held throughout the United States.

• **Representative democracy:** Citizens elect officials to act on their behalf. If the officeholders disappoint or anger them, the citizens can choose new officials at the next election. A regime that runs by representative democracy is known as a **republic.** In a republic, citizens hold the power. There are two major types of representative democracies:

» **Parliamentary democracy:** Citizens elect officials to act as legislators. The legislature then elects the executive (frequently called the prime minister) from its members

> *EXAMPLE:* Many European democracies use a parliamentary system. One advantage of this type of democracy is its ability to quickly respond to public opinion. If the prime minister loses the confidence of voters, new elections can be held immediately. But parliamentary governments can be unstable. Perhaps the classic example is Italy, which changed governments about once a year for fifty years following World War II.

» **Presidential democracy:** Citizens elect the legislators and executive separately. No one can be both a legislator and the executive at the same time.

> *EXAMPLE:* The United States is a presidential democracy. Although a presidential system can be slow to respond to changes in public opinion, it is likely to be more stable than a parliamentary system.

CHAPTER 1

STRENGTHS AND WEAKNESSES OF DEMOCRACIES		
	Direct Democracy	**Representative Democracy**
Strengths	Most purely democratic form of government because the people literally rule	Can take place in a much larger country; grants citizens much more time to pursue private interests
Weaknesses	Difficult to form except in small communities; demands constant attention from its citizens	Can be slow to respond to public opinion; sometimes defies public opinion

Key Features of a Democracy

All democracies, in theory, should provide four basic things:

- **Security:** Like all governments, a democracy should protect its citizens from danger and threats, both national and abroad.

- **Liberty:** A democracy bestows on its citizens the right to do certain things without interference. The most common liberties are freedom of speech, thought, religion, and assembly. Most democratic governments are **limited**—that is, there are fundamental rights that the government cannot take from its citizens.

- **Political equality:** All citizens should be treated the same way. Each person gets one vote in elections, and the law is the same for all people.

- **Popular sovereignty:** In a democracy, supreme power rests with the people. The people choose their government, and the people can change the government when they see fit. In return, the government should do what the people want.

In reality, these features do not always fit together well, and democracies must work to create a balance. But the balance changes as the people decide they want to emphasize one feature over another. Sometimes strengthening one feature causes another feature to decrease or to disappear.

Liberty vs. Security

For the most part, Americans tend to value liberty more than anything else. However, since the attacks of September 11, 2001, Americans have become more concerned with issues of security. In response, the government has increased security by limiting some freedoms—making it easier for the government to investigate its citizens, for instance.

Sources of Political Power

Where does political power come from? Scholars have developed two models to explain the source of political power:

1. **Percolation-up model:** Political power rests with the citizens. In turn, citizens grant political power to their leaders through elections. This view appeals to our democratic sensibilities, but it may not be correct. After all, throughout most of human history—and in many parts of the world today—strong and stable governments ignored their citizens.

2. **Drip-down model:** Political power rests with the leaders, who organize society and impose order. Nevertheless, citizens retain the power to overthrow the government by electing new leaders.

Political scientists use both of these views in different circumstances. Sometimes change happens in a society because of a genuine grassroots effort. In other cases, government leaders create a policy and impose it on the people. And sometimes both happen.

> ### The Models in Action
>
> The civil rights movement in the United States had elements of both percolation-up and drip-down models of power. Much of the original push for the movement came from African Americans, who were angry about their status as second-class citizens. They organized and staged a variety of protests to bring about change—an example of the percolation-up model in action. After it became apparent that many state governments (especially, but not only, in the South) would resist giving African Americans equal rights, the federal government began asserting its power to enforce laws and court decisions—an example of the drip-down model in action.

Sources of Political Legitimacy

All governments need legitimacy to survive. But how do governments attain authority? What makes citizens obey or feel loyal toward their governments? Scholars have answered these questions by concluding that political legitimacy comes from several sources:

- **Tradition:** The government has authority because its citizens have a long tradition of giving it authority and respect. This source mostly comes into play with governments that have been around for a long time.

- **Habit:** Most people are raised to obey the laws, and they thereby acquire the habit of obeying. Citizens give their government legitimacy and authority because that is what they have always done.

- **History:** People remember great deeds and events in the country's history, and they obey the government out of a sense of historical pride.

- **Religion:** In some places, obedience to the government is seen as a religious obligation.

  > *EXAMPLE:* Iran is a constitutional Islamic republic. Some of its governing bodies are elected, whereas others are put into place for religious reasons.

- **Ethnic identity:** Countries composed of exclusively one ethnic group or whose regime is strongly connected to one ethnic group can inspire obedience through ethnic identity. Members of that ethnic group respect the government because of its link to their ethnicity.

  > *EXAMPLE:* Saddam Hussein's Sunni regime in Iraq once inspired a great deal of loyalty in Sunni Arabs.

- **Results:** If a government succeeds in some way—for instance, through a military victory or a thriving economy—citizens may feel loyalty because of that success.

- **Elections:** A government that holds elections gains legitimacy because citizens believe that the government, composed of elected officials, represents them.

- **International recognition:** A government gains legitimacy when other governments recognize it and welcome it to the international community.

CHAPTER 1

EXAMPLE: The United States and many European countries moved quickly to publicly recognize the controversial new nation-state of Israel when it was created in 1948. Although most countries formally recognize Israel and the Israeli government today, Iran and many Arab countries still do not, which is one reason why the Middle East remains such a hot spot in global politics.

Taiwan, an island that was under Chinese control up until the end of World War II, still has not received formal recognition as a nation-state to this day. Not even the United States has formally recognized Taiwan, fearing that doing so would sour American relations with China, which still claims the island. As a result, the people and government of Taiwan have lived in fear that no other country would help them if China tried to retake control of the island by force.

Sample Test Questions

1. What is politics?

2. What is political science?

3. Describe the origins and evolution of political science.

4. What is authority?

    A. The ultimate power in society
    B. A government ruled by a few
    C. The branch of government that enforces the law.
    D. A government's ability to exercise power without resorting to force.

5. Which of the following is the same as a monarchy?

A. Dictatorship
B. Parliamentary government
C. Anarchy
D. Aristocracy

6. Totalitarian government is one extreme type of government. Which of the following is at the other end of the political spectrum?

A. Dictatorship
B. Parliamentary government
C. Anarchy
D. Aristocracy

7. What is the difference between direct and representative democracy?

A. The amount of freedom citizens have
B. Elected legislators
C. A king
D. Rule of the people

8. What is the difference between parliamentary and presidential democracy?

A. Election of the executive branch
B. Election of the legislature
C. The court system
D. Extent of government power

9. In the percolation-up model, where does political power come from?

A. The ruling class
B. The people
C. The constitution
D. Religion

10. Which of the following is *not* a source of legitimacy?

A. Tradition
B. Habit
C. Sovereignty
D. Ethnicity

ANSWERS

1. Politics is the process by which government decisions are made.

2. Political science is the systematic study of politics.

3. Political science originated in ancient Greece, with philosophers such as Plato and Aristotle. In the early modern era, thinkers such as Hobbes began to apply the methods of mathematics and science to the study of politics. This trend continued into the nineteenth century with the breakthroughs in sociology of Marx and Weber. In the twentieth century, political scientists have adopted a number of approaches, including the use of statistical analysis.

4. D

5. A

6. C

7. B

8. A

9. B

10. C

Suggested Reading

- Hobbes, Thomas. *Leviathan,* edited by C. B. MacPherson. New York: Penguin Classics, 1982.

Using the methods of geometry, Hobbes breaks down the state into its parts. He then rebuilds the state into a model of a good state, which must be absolute.

- Locke, John. *Second Treatise of Government,* edited by Thomas P. Peardon. New York: Prentice Hall, 1952.

Locke's book is in many ways the founding document of modern liberal democracy.

- Machiavelli, Niccolo. *The Prince.* Harvey Mansfield, trans. 2nd ed. Chicago: University of Chicago Press, 1998.

Notorious for its brutality, this book imagines politics as a bloody contest in which success is the only goal.

- Madison, James, Alexander Hamilton, and John Jay. *The Federalist,* edited by J. R. Poole. Indianapolis: Hackett, 2005.

This book provides insights into the nature of politics and the reasoning behind the Constitution of the United States.

- Marx, Karl, and Friedrich Engels. *The Communist Manifesto.* Translated by Martin Malia. 1848. Reprint, New York: Signet Classics, 1998.

This book presents a very different view of politics, one that renounces liberal democracy as nothing more than the tool of the wealthy.

- Mill, John Stuart. *On Liberty*. New York: Penguins Classics, 1975.

In this work, Mill presents a powerful argument for expansive freedom in society.

- Plato. *The Republic*. Translated by G. M. A. Grube and C. D. C. Reeve. 2nd ed. Indianapolis: Hackett, 1992.

Plato's most famous political dialogue focuses on the creation of a good society.

- Simpson, Peter, ed. *The Politics of Aristotle*. Chapel Hill: University of North Carolina Press, 1997.

Aristotle's important work is the first attempt to systematize knowledge of government.

Useful Websites

- www.apsanet.org

The website of the American Political Science Association, the leading organization of political scientists in the United States.

- www.freedomehouse.org

An organization that measures and promotes democracy around the world.

- www.gutenberg.org

A great source for free ebooks; many classics of political theory can be found there.

- www.lib.umich.edu/govdocs/polisci.html

The University of Michigan is one of the leading political science schools in the United States; this page has many links to sites that might interest or help those studying politics.

POLITICAL IDEOLOGIES AND STYLES

2

Overview

Our ideologies shape the way we perceive the world. People with different ideologies see things quite differently. A person with a pessimistic ideology, for example, might see every person he passes on the street as a potential thief and liar. But someone with an optimistic view of human nature will view those same people on the street as potential friends. This phenomenon occurs in politics as well: Our ideologies shape how we see, hear, and analyze political discourse.

Ideologies also influence our behavior and how we make decisions. In politics, ideology often determines whom we vote for. Generally, conservatives tend to vote for Republican candidates, and liberals tend to vote for Democratic candidates. But our attitudes also help determine whether we will donate money to candidates, go to rallies, and even vote. On a larger, more global scale, ideologies often heavily influence political parties, leaders, and policy. People's firm belief in their ideologies has led them to cause wars, found countries, ignite revolutions, wage genocide, and create empires. As a result, understanding the various major political ideologies that have shaped much of Western history is fundamental to understanding political science. Likewise, understanding the differences in American political ideologies helps us better understand the American people and government.

What Is an Ideology?

An **ideology** is a set of beliefs that affects our outlook on the world. Our ideology is our most closely held set of values and feelings, and it acts as the filter through which we see everything and everybody. In fact, these beliefs are often so close to us that we do not realize that they are there. We simply think that our beliefs are natural and obviously true. Religion is one type of ideology, and religious belief affects a person's views.

CHARACTERISTICS OF AN IDEOLOGY

Ideologies can vary greatly in the following ways:

- **Complexity:** Some ideologies are very simple, whereas others, such as Marxism, are quite detailed.

  > *EXAMPLE:* "Don't trust anybody over 30!" was a simple ideology held by many young Americans in the 1960s.

- **Consistency:** Sometimes the ideas that constitute a single ideology conflict with one another. Similarly, sometimes a person's views shift significantly over time.

  > *EXAMPLE:* Benito Mussolini, the father of Italian fascism, was a communist when he was younger. The fact that fascism was strongly anticommunist never seemed to bother him.

- **Flexibility:** Some elaborate ideologies, like some religious beliefs, allow almost no wiggle room and have answers to all questions. Other ideologies have a great deal of flexibility.

  > *EXAMPLE:* The Catholic Catechism, which details the beliefs of the Catholic Church, is thousands of pages long and covers almost every topic imaginable. There is little room for individual interpretation. In contrast, the ideology of libertarianism encourages individuals to make decisions for themselves.

CHAPTER 2

Major Political Ideologies

Over the millennia, political philosophers have expounded on a variety of political ideologies, or ways governments and societies can be organized. Today, scholars generally talk about five major political ideologies:

1. Anarchism

2. Absolutism

3. Liberalism

4. Conservatism

5. Socialism

These political ideologies are, for the most part, mutually exclusive. So, a liberal government does not usually practice socialism, nor does an absolute ruler follow liberalism. The five major political ideologies have played a key role in history by shaping governments and political movements.

ANARCHISM

The belief that the best government is absolutely no government is known as **anarchism.** This ideology argues that everything about governments is repressive and therefore must be abolished entirely. A related ideology known as **nihilism** emphasizes that everything—both government and society—must be periodically destroyed in order to start anew. Nihilists often categorically reject traditional concepts of morality in favor of violence and terror. Anarchism and nihilism were once associated with socialism because many anarchists and nihilists supported the socialists' call for revolution and the complete overhaul of government and society in the early to mid-twentieth century.

EXAMPLE: Although neither violent nor strictly anarchist, members of the American Libertarian Party believe that government should be so small that it hardly ever interferes in citizens' lives, thereby best preserving individual liberty.

Russia

Russia has had a long association with anarchism and nihilism. Many prominent members of both movements were Russian, including Mikhail Bakunin, considered the father of anarchism. Russian nihilists engaged in a number of terrorist attacks in the late nineteenth and early twentieth centuries, including the assassination of Czar Alexander II in 1881.

ABSOLUTISM

Traditionally, much of Western civilization's history was dominated by **absolutism,** the belief that a single ruler should have control over every aspect of the government and of the people's lives. Absolute rulers had a variety of titles, including *chieftain, king, shah, pharaoh, emperor, sultan,* and *prince.* In some cultures, the absolute ruler was seen as a god in human form. Other peoples believed that their ruler had the **divine right of kings,** meaning that God had chosen the ruler to govern the rest. As a result, many cultures with absolute rulers practiced some form of **caesaropapism,** the belief that the ruler is head of both the governmental authority and the religious authority.

EXAMPLE: In the Byzantine Empire, the double-headed eagle symbolized caesaropapism. The two heads stood for church and state. This symbol clearly and graphically portrayed the unity of religious and secular power in one person.

Advocates of Absolutism

A number of political philosophers have advocated absolutism. The Greek philosopher Plato, for example, firmly believed that the best government would be run by a benevolent absolute ruler who would have the people's best interests at heart. English philosopher Thomas Hobbes, meanwhile, was perhaps the most persuasive proponent of absolutism. In his book *Leviathan* (1651), he argued that life without governments was "nasty, brutish, and short" and that people must willingly submit to absolute rulers—even tyrannical ones—in order to live longer, more stable lives.

Absolutist Beliefs

Absolutism emphasizes:

- **A strong sense of order:** Everything should be carefully structured, including society. Disorder and chaos are generally considered to be dangerous.

- **A clear-cut law of nature (or law of God):** This law must be obeyed. According to this law, some people are inherently better than others. A natural **hierarchy** (a power structure in which some people have authority over others) exists. Therefore, the superior should rule the inferior. This general view is called **elitism,** or **elite theory.**

- **The wisdom of traditional values and institutions:** New ideas are considered dangerous to the order of things.

LIBERALISM

In the early modern age of the Western world (beginning roughly in the early 1500s and running for about 200 years), a number of changes occurred that led to new ideologies: The European discovery of the Americas, the rise of Protestantism, the beginnings of the free-market economy, and the early stages of the scientific revolution fundamentally altered Europe. People began developing different ways of thinking to take account of these changes.

Perhaps the most important of the new ideas is **liberalism** (also known as **classical liberalism**). This type of liberalism, which began in England in the 1600s, differs from American liberalism. Classical liberalism developed when such thinkers as John Locke (in his *Second Treatise of Government* in 1690) rethought the relationship between the individual and society, as well theorized about the rights and responsibilities of the individual. These ideas formed the foundation for many political systems still operating today.

Liberalism in Action

During the French Revolution (1789–1799), the monarchy and much of the church were destroyed, as were traditional laws and habits in different parts of the country. The revolutionaries exalted reason, to the point of literally creating a temple to it (the revolutionaries renamed the Church of Notre Dame in Paris "the Temple of Reason") in 1793. But as a result of the revolution, France plunged into years of civil war and violence. Only the emergence of Napoleon—an authoritarian ruler—brought stability back to the country.

Liberal Beliefs

Liberalism emphasizes:

- **Individualism:** The individual takes priority over society.

- **Freedom:** Individuals have the right to make choices for themselves. This freedom is not absolute, and some behaviors, such as murder, are prohibited. Freedom of religion is a particularly important freedom to come out of liberalism because so many governments at the time were very closely tied to a particular religious creed.

- **Equality:** No person is morally or politically superior to others. Hierarchies are rejected.

- **Rationalism:** Humans are capable of thinking logically and rationally. Logic and reason help us solve problems.

- **Progress:** Traditions should not be kept unless they have value. New ideas are helpful because they can lead to progress in the sciences, the economy, and society.

- **The free market:** Liberalism and capitalism go hand in hand. Liberals like the free market because it more easily creates wealth, as opposed to traditional economies, which often have extensive regulations and limits on which occupations people can hold.

These basic characteristics of liberalism have led liberals to argue in favor of a limited government, which draws its power from the people. In practice, this has meant favoring a democratic government.

Mill's Good Government

In his books *On Liberty* (1859) and *Considerations of Representative Government* (1861), English philosopher J. S. Mill argued that good governments should be unrestricting enough to allow people—both men *and* women—to pursue their own interests and achieve their own potential as they see fit. Fostering individuality would, in turn, benefit society as a whole, because fewer people would feel restricted or marginalized. Mill also believed that representative democracy was the best form of government because it allowed people to express their individuality and provided them the opportunity to take a more active role in the political process. The more active the people are, Mill thought, the more satisfied they are with their government.

Classical liberalism has profoundly influenced the modern world, so much so that we do not even realize how controversial its ideas were in early modern Europe. Back then, liberal ideas were considered dangerous and inflammatory by traditional European governments, and liberals were frequently persecuted. Even after liberalism took hold in England, the rest of Europe was hostile to liberal ideas for another century (and even longer in some cases).

EXAMPLE: For centuries, Eastern Europe suffered greatly from authoritarian rule, in which one person or a small group holds all the political power and oppresses everybody else. As recently as 1989, open discussion of liberal ideas (such as the free market) or publicly complaining that the communist governments did not speak for the people could get a person arrested. The writer Vaclav Havel, for example, was jailed by the Czechoslovakian government. But after the 1989 end of the communist government in Czecho-slovakia, Havel served as the newly democratic government's first president.

The Controversial Case of John Locke

In the seventeenth century, liberals were not held in high esteem, as evidenced by the life of John Locke. Locke was forced to flee into exile to avoid arrest by the British monarchy. He returned to England only after the Stuart monarchs were overthrown in 1688 and a government friendlier to liberalism took power. But even then, Locke refused to acknowledge that he had written *Second Treatise of Government,* his main political text, because of its controversial nature. Other liberals, in England and elsewhere, were arrested or even killed by traditional governments.

CONSERVATISM

Conservatism (also known as **classical conservatism**) began as a reaction against the liberal ideas taking hold of Europe during the French Revolution in the late eighteenth century. This type of conservatism differs from American conservatism. Edmund Burke, a British member of Parliament, observed the early stages of the French Revolution with great distress and predicted the violence and terror that would ensue. His book, *Reflections on the Revolution in France* (1790), is one of the founding texts of classical conservatism.

Burke and other conservatives attacked liberalism for many reasons. They argued that liberalism destroyed tradition. In its rush to overturn the old and bring in the new, liberalism and capitalism ruthlessly attacked traditional institutions and beliefs.

Conservative Beliefs

Conservatism emphasizes:

- **Stability:** Stability is a precious thing, and change must be made gradually in order to preserve it. Undermining stability is very dangerous because societies can easily fall into chaos and violence. Classical liberals frequently called for revolution, which opens the door to great turbulence, according to the classical conservative view.

- **Concreteness:** Liberalism is too abstract. It focuses on freedom and equality, not on the concrete way people live every day.

- **Human fallibility:** Liberalism overestimates human beings. Humans are frequently ignorant, prejudiced, and irrational. By ignoring these defects, liberalism becomes unrealistic.

- **Unique circumstances:** There is no universal answer to the problems of society; the circumstances are unique in each country.

Classical Conservatism and Democracy

Many early conservatives favored authoritarian government. In the aftermath of the Napoleonic Wars (roughly 1792–1815), for example, most European governments actively worked to stop the spread of liberalism and democracy. Nevertheless, conservatives were not necessarily hostile to democracy. Generally these conservatives argued that some sort of monarchy was necessary, but some were more open to popular government. Burke, in particular, thought that limited democracy was a good form of government for England, as long as it maintained the customs and mores it inherited from its predecessors.

Classical Conservatism Today

For the most part, classical conservatism has faded. Most people who label themselves conservatives are more like American conservatives than classical ones. But there are still some classical conservatives. Many of them in Europe have ties to old noble families, and some advocate monarchism. Classical conservatives can also be found in other parts of the world.

The chart below compares classical liberal views with classical conservative views on several issues.

CLASSICAL LIBERALISM VERSUS CLASSICAL CONSERVATISM		
Issue	**Liberalism**	**Conservatism**
Tradition	Only valuable if it serves a purpose; we should not be afraid to overturn tradition	Repository of acquired wisdom; collection of best knowledge from many years of practice
Freedom	Essential for human flourishing; people are free to do as they please as long as they do not hurt others	Excessive freedom is bad; lets people ignore societal responsibilities and overlook social customs
Reason	Relies on reason; the great success of the scientific revolution can be repeated in human affairs if we use reason	Thinks reason is fallible and prone to error; human beings cannot discover the best way to govern through thinking. Instead, we must base our judgments and decisions on experience.
Free Market	Valuable because it unleashes tremendous economic growth and efficiency, enriching society	Dangerous because it breaks down traditional economic roles. The profit motive corrodes customary mores and reduces all relationships to cash transactions.

CHAPTER 2

SOCIALISM

Socialism arose as a response to the Industrial Revolution, which was the emergence of technologies such as the steam engine and mass production. The Industrial Revolution started in England in the last years of the eighteenth century and had spread to much of Europe and America by the end of the nineteenth century. It caused major upheavals: In a very short time, many people were forced to abandon agricultural ways of life for the modern mechanized world of factories.

Early versions of socialism were put forward in Europe in the first part of the nineteenth century (these versions are often dubbed "utopian socialism"), but truly influential socialist theories did not emerge until industrialization expanded in the mid-nineteenth century. Karl Marx is the best-known theorist of socialism. Along with Friedrich Engels, Marx wrote *The Communist Manifesto* (1848) as a call to revolution. Other prominent socialists thinkers included Karl Kautsky, Vladimir Lenin, and Antonio Gramsci.

Socialist Beliefs
Socialism emphasizes:

- **Collectivism:** Human beings are social by nature, and society should respect this. Individualism is poisonous.

- **Public ownership:** Society, not individuals, should own the property.

- **Central economic planning:** The government plans the economy; there is no free market.

- **Economic equality:** All citizens have roughly the same level of prosperity.

Class Warfare
According to socialists, liberalism fails to live up to its promises of freedom and equality. Socialists blame the free market for liberalism's failings. Under a capitalist system, money and

means of production are the measures of power. The haves (the *bourgeoisie,* in Marx's terms) and the have-nots (whom Marx calls the *proletariat*) are locked into a fight that Marx called *class warfare.* Because they control the money and means of production, the bourgeoisie have the power and thus are winning the fight. The rich use the government to further their control and to increase their power over the lower, poorer classes, so people are neither free nor equal.

The Evolution of Socialism

Socialism evolved in a variety of ways. Communism and democratic socialism are the two most prominent evolutions of socialism.

- **Communism:** An authoritarian and revolutionary approach to achieving socialism. As an ideology, communism emphasizes a classless society in which all members jointly share the means and output of production. The regimes of the Soviet Union and communist China embody this ideology. Communists such as Vladimir Lenin, who became the first premier of the Soviet Union in 1917, argued that people can and must make the transition to socialism quickly rather than waiting for it to evolve. Authoritarian and violent measures are often required because the defenders of capitalism will fight ferociously to stop socialism from coming into being.

Communism Today

With the fall of communist regimes in Russia and Eastern Europe, communism has been in retreat for most of the 1990s and 2000s. There are, for example, fewer communist movements around the world than during the Cold War. But there are still several major communist regimes, including the governments of North Korea and Cuba.

- **Democratic socialism:** A peaceful and democratic approach to achieving socialism. As an ideology, democratic socialism also emphasizes a classless society in which all members jointly share the means and output of production. But unlike communism, democratic socialism attempts to achieve its goals peacefully via the democratic processes. Democratic socialists reject the need for immediate transition to socialism in favor of a gradualist approach, achieved by working within a democratic government. Economic inequalities should be remedied through a **welfare state,** a system that provides aid to the poor and help to the unemployed.

Democratic Socialism Today

Democratic socialism has been quite successful in western Europe and Scandinavia. Many governments there have extensive welfare systems that have remained largely intact even when democratic socialists are voted out of office. Democratic socialist parties exist in many democracies around the world. Germany's Social Democratic Party and Britain's Labor Party are contemporary examples of successful political parties heavily influenced by democratic socialism.

Political Styles

States and political leaders use a variety of political styles to further the interests of the state, including:

- Nationalism
- Fascism
- Fundamentalism

Political scientists debate whether these styles constitute distinct ideologies in and of themselves. On the one hand, these styles are not as well codified or philosophically grounded as the five political ideologies previously discussed (anarchism, absolutism, liberalism, conservatism, and socialism). On the other hand, each has played a key role in shaping events in world history generally and twentieth-century governments specifically. Keep in mind that these styles and the five political ideologies are not mutually exclusive, so a government may be nationalist and liberal or nationalist, fascist, and conservative.

NATIONALISM

Nationalism, a strong belief that one's nation is great (and, usually, better than others), also arose during the modern era. In the eighteenth and nineteenth centuries, nationalism emerged as a powerful force that caused a number of revolutions. People began to identify with and take pride in their particular nation-state. The French Revolution and the subsequent Napoleonic Wars helped spread nationalism throughout Europe because many nations rallied together to defeat Napoleon.

> ### Democracy and Nationalism
>
> In some ways, nationalism works best in a democratic society. Nationalism is a popular movement because it has the potential to appeal to all citizens, and rallying large numbers of people together is necessary for a democratic society to function. Historically, many democratic states have prompted strong nationalist sentiments. France before and during World War I (1914–1918) was fiercely nationalist. The United States is also strongly nationalist.

Nationalist Beliefs

Nationalists believe that being a member of a particular nation is wonderful and worthy of celebration. For example, one should honor one's "Frenchness" if from France or "Americanness" if from the United States. This belief is not tied to any one political system. Nationalists favor behavior, governmental systems, and other values or behaviors that promote a strong nation, including a powerful economy, a strong military, and unity among citizens. Threats to the nation are taken very seriously and need to be addressed. Historically, there have been many authoritarian regimes, in which governments may do whatever they want, that were strongly nationalist in character, but there are plenty of democratic nationalist states as well. The means of promoting a strong nation vary greatly from one nationalist state to another.

CHAPTER 2

EXAMPLE: The 2006 World Cup in Germany gave political scientists the opportunity to watch a democratic country become more nationalist. After World War II, Germans largely refrained from outwardly demonstrating any sense of nationalism, a result of lingering guilt over Nazism and the Holocaust. But the success of the German soccer team prompted many citizens to begin feeling strong nationalist pride for the first time in decades, including proudly displaying the German flag.

FASCISM

Fascism is a highly nationalist, militaristic, totalitarian political ideology in which one person has absolute power. World War I was the key event that spawned fascism. The war was the first major war fought between industrialized nations, which were armed with technology such as machine guns and chemical weapons. The result was utter devastation. Millions died, entire countries collapsed, and those who survived were often profoundly disillusioned. For many people, the war showed that modern ideas had failed and that a new way was needed.

Fascism arose in Italy in the 1920s. Italy had fought on the winning side of World War I, but it had suffered greatly. Many Italians were angry and disappointed that the country gained very little for the price it paid. Some war veterans felt alienated from society: They had grown accustomed to the horrors of war, and now normal life seemed unreal and incomprehensible. Some of these war veterans began to rally together, trying to re-create the camaraderie of the war. Their meetings led to the development of fascism. In its original form, fascism was neither racist nor anti-Semitic. Indeed, some early Italian fascists were Jewish.

Although Italy was the birthplace of fascism, this -ism spread to other countries. In the mid- to late twentieth century, the Spanish government under General Francisco Franco was fascist, as were the Argentinean government under Juan Perón and some of the governments in Eastern Europe before World-War II. The Japanese government before and during World War II also shared some fascist ideas.

Fascist Beliefs

Fascism emphasizes:

- **Action:** Human beings find meaning and purpose by acting, not by reasoning or thinking.

- **Community spirit:** People need to be part of a community. Individualism is dangerous because it turns people away from their community.

- **Nationalism:** The community that matters the most is the nation. People should work together to promote the glory and power of the nation.

- **Militarism:** The nation must have a strong, powerful military. The nation shows its power by expanding its territory.

- **The future:** Fascists love the speed and power of technology. They look optimistically to the future.

- **One party:** The nation must be unified and speak with one voice. Therefore, only one political party is allowed, and that party rules with absolute power.

- **Violence:** The government rules its people through violence or the threat of violence.

Nazism

Nazism is a particular variety of fascism that combines elements of anticommunism, racism, and anti-Semitism. In the 1920s, Nazism arose in Germany as a result of its defeat in World War I. The Treaty of Versailles, which ended the war in 1918, imposed harsh sanctions on Germany. Many Germans felt humiliated and angry. The economic disaster of the Great Depression a few years later added to their sense of despair. Nazism appealed to many of these people because it offered meaning, hope, and solutions. Nazis came to power in the early 1930s in Germany, led by Adolf Hitler. Its aggressive foreign policy led to the start of World War II in 1939. Although Nazism was defeated and discredited with the German defeat in the war, some groups around the world are still influenced by this ideology.

Nazism shares a number of things with fascism, including strong nationalist sentiment, a focus on community, and the value it places on action, militarism, and authoritarian government. But Nazism differs from fascism in two significant ways:

- **Belief in a mythical past:** Nazism looks back to a mythical past for inspiration. German Nazis saw themselves as heirs to the Teutonic knights of medieval Europe, fighting against evil for the good of the German people.

- **Racial purity:** A core part of Nazism is virulent racism. In particular, German Nazis hated Jews, blaming them for all of the evils of the world. But other groups, including Slavs and gypsies, were also considered inferior and fit only for slave labor. This racist belief led to the Holocaust, in which millions of Jews, Slavs, gentiles, and others were killed in a Nazi attempt to "purify" Europe.

FUNDAMENTALISM

In its most basic meaning, **fundamentalism** is the belief that a religious text is absolutely and literally true and that anything opposing the text must be wrong. All behavior and belief must be guided by this central text, and anything else is sinful. Scholars use the terms *fundamentalism* and *fundamentalist* to describe some religions.

Nearly all religions have fundamentalist believers or sects. In the United States, for example, Christian fundamentalists constitute a powerful portion of the population. These people (sometimes referred to as the Religious Right, Christian Right, or Christian Conservatives) have had a major impact on American politics, especially in the Republican Party.

> **Fundamentalism in Action**
>
> In recent years, Americans, Europeans, and secular Middle Easterners have been attacked by Islamic fundamentalists. These fundamentalists believe that Islam is the only true religion, that the Koran is absolutely and literally true, and that the Middle East should return to a single Islamic state. Most Muslims are not fundamentalist, but the fundamentalist extremists have had a huge impact on global politics since 2001.

CHAPTER 2

American Ideologies

American political ideologies are variations on classical liberalism. As a result, these ideologies tend to be very similar: Almost everyone in the United States, for example, believes in limited government, the free market, and individual liberty. Democrats just happen to lean slightly to the left and Republicans slightly to the right. Differences arise between these two groups because each party has a slightly different opinion on how best to achieve these goals. American political ideologies, like all others, are not monolithic. Republicans frequently disagree with other Republicans, and Democrats frequently disagree with other Democrats. In the end, however, members of both parties share very similar core beliefs, unlike members of political parties in most other countries.

Political scientists sometimes organize the four major American political ideologies with respect to their preference for the size and influence of the political government. Libertarians favor almost no government at all, whereas socialists, at the other end of the spectrum, favor a high degree of government intervention. At the center of the spectrum, American liberals and conservatives represent a balance of the two extremes. Note that adherents to all four ideologies still favor representative democratic governments.

AMERICAN LIBERALISM

American liberalism argues that the government needs to act to ensure equality among its citizens. Historically, for example, liberal groups worked to promote civil rights for African Americans and other minorities. In current politics, many liberals are pushing for gay rights, affirmative action, open immigration, and similar policies.

American Liberal Beliefs

Generally, liberals push for social, political, and economic equality, as well as expansive civil liberties. Liberals generally want the government to help the poor and make sure that the rich do not have too much power. Although they support capitalism, liberals do not want a completely free market; some government action is needed to ameliorate the worst aspects of the market. Therefore, liberals tend to favor:

- Graduated income taxes that tax the wealthier more than the poor

- Welfare programs to aid the poor

- Major government spending on education

- Job-retraining programs for unemployed workers

- Action to promote equal opportunity

- Expanded civil liberties

The chart on the following page lists the different views held by liberals and conservatives on a variety of issues. Of course, individual beliefs transcend general categories: Some conservatives are pro-choice, some liberals are anti–gun control, and some liberals and conservatives might not have strongly held views on any of those issues.

LIBERAL VIEWS VERSUS CONSERVATIVE VIEWS		
Issue	Liberal View	Conservative View
Abortion	Legal and open to all women	Immoral and should be banned
Gun control	Heavy restrictions	Few restrictions
Taxes	Higher, progressive	Lower, flatter
Affirmative action	Necessary to make up for centuries of discrimination	Unfair because it reversely favors some and excludes others
Gay marriage	Should be legal	Should be illegal

We sometimes think of conservatives as being stronger on national defense than liberals, but this is not always true. During the twentieth century, conservative and liberal leaders worked to strengthen the American military and sometimes engaged in war. For instance, in the 1960s and 1970s, John F. Kennedy increased military spending dramatically, and Lyndon Johnson greatly expanded America's role in the Vietnam War.

How a Liberal Becomes a Conservative

There are many adages about how belief changes. For example, one adage states that a conservative is a liberal who has been mugged, while a liberal is a conservative who has lost his or her job. Winston Churchill is said to have remarked, "Any twenty-year-old who isn't a liberal doesn't have a heart, and any forty-year-old who isn't a conservative doesn't have a brain."

CHAPTER 2

AMERICAN CONSERVATISM

American conservatism argues that the government's main job is to protect freedom and provide security. Beyond that, the government should stay out of people's lives and should allow people to do, act, and behave as they see fit. According to conservatives, freedom trumps equality: The government should promote the former, regardless of how expanded freedoms might affect equality.

American Conservative Beliefs

Conservatives argue that the best way to achieve prosperity is for the government to stay out of the economy. Taxes should be low and regulation minimal so that the market can work most efficiently. Although the government should not ignore the plight of the poor, the best way to help the poor is to give them opportunities to better themselves. Conservatives tend to:

- Believe strongly in tradition, particularly religious tradition

- Support traditional notions of family

- Oppose gay marriage and abortion

- Favor lower taxes

- Support states' rights

- Favor a strong military and aggressive foreign policies

Neoconservatism

In recent years, the term **neoconservative** has emerged to describe one branch of American conservatism. A neoconservative believes in using the government to actively work to achieve conservative goals. Although most neoconservatives still favor a small government, they argue that the government must act assertively in some areas to promote conservative values and policies.

Neoconservatives and the Iraq War

Even before George W. Bush was elected in 2000, a number of neoconservatives pushed for an invasion of Iraq to oust Saddam Hussein. William Kristol, editor of *The Weekly Standard,* had argued for such a war as early as 1998. When Bush came into office, he appointed a number of neoconservatives to key government positions, including Paul Wolfowitz as assistant secretary of defense. Many critics of the Bush Administration have complained that the Iraq War was started because of the ideological zeal of the neoconservatives. Some have even referred to the war as "Kristol's War" because of the role William Kristol had in promoting it.

CHAPTER 2

AMERICAN LIBERTARIANISM

A smaller but equally important American ideology is **libertarianism.** Libertarians believe that personal liberty trumps all other considerations. Therefore, according to libertarianism, the government should stay out of people's lives as much as possible. So libertarians want the government to lower taxes, reduce its size dramatically, and literally leave people alone. Some people advocate controversial positions, such as the legalization of drugs, abolishing income taxes, and ending all welfare programs. Libertarians are few in number, but they have exercised important influences on American politics.

EXAMPLE: Libertarian ideals contributed to the founding of the American Civil Liberties Union (ACLU), which has played a key role in monitoring what it sees as excessive government power, in the early twentieth century. Although the ACLU is not, strictly speaking, a libertarian organization, some of its views are very libertarian in nature. On the other side, the Cato Institute is a conservative think tank with very strong libertarian views. Both groups have shaped policy and society for decades.

Both liberals and conservatives attack libertarianism. Liberals want the government to play an active role in the economy, whereas conservatives do not want to extend freedom to behavior such as drug use. Libertarians are neither liberal nor conservative, and they essentially differ from anarchists in that libertarians want a very limited government, whereas anarchists want no government.

AMERICAN SOCIALISM

American socialists advocate strong federal leadership and centralization of the economy in order to provide the greatest public good by benefiting as many citizens as possible. Most socialists in American are democratic socialists who want to preserve the American tradition of representative government, although there a number of small communist parties in the United States that still believe revolution is necessary in order to overthrow the capitalist order.

> EXAMPLE: The turn of the twentieth century was the golden age for American socialism. Hundreds of thousands of impoverished midwestern farmers fought for increased federal intervention in the economy to regulate big business. Political activist Eugene V. Debs ran for president several times on the Socialist Party ticket—and at one point, he waged his campaign from jail. In the 1920 presidential election, Debs won nearly a million popular votes.

American conservatives and liberals alike attack socialism because of the nation's history of fighting communism during the Cold War and because socialism challenges the belief in the free-market economy. Nevertheless, proponents of socialism have influenced mainstream American politics a number of times, most notably during the Great Depression, when President Franklin Roosevelt and Democrats in Congress passed a variety of New Deal bills aimed at helping the poorest Americans.

Feminism and Environmentalism

Two American political ideologies have gained momentum in recent years. **Feminism** is the belief that women are equal to men and should be treated equally by the law. Thus far, feminists have not yet banded together into one distinct political party. **Environmentalism** is the belief that we have an obligation to protect the world from the excesses of human occupation. Environmentalists are represented by the Green Party, which has won elections in Alaska, Arizona, Connecticut, Florida, Iowa, Minnesota, and Pennsylvania, among other states.

Sample Test Questions

1. What is an ideology? Why are ideologies important?

2. Define fundamentalism.

3. Describe the core elements of classical liberalism. Name at least one key figure in the founding of liberalism.

4. American conservatism differs in many ways from traditional conservatism. Describe those differences.

5. Socialism can be characterized as an attempt to make good on the failed promises of liberalism. Why is this?

6. Which belief best describes nationalism?

    A. The belief in the innate goodness of the individual
    B. The belief that one's nation is great
    C. The belief that inequalities in the economy destroy any equality in politics
    D. The belief that one person is chosen by God to rule over the rest

7. American liberalism differs from classical liberalism in which way?

    A. A stress on political equality
    B. Opposition to absolute government
    C. Support for government intervention in the economy
    D. A belief in individual dignity

8. Which of the following is *not* a shared belief of fascism and Nazism?

    A. Racism
    B. Nationalism
    C. Militarism
    D. Authoritarianism

9. Libertarians would support which of the following policies?

    A. Increased taxes to pay for public education
    B. Strengthening the military
    C. Increasing funding for health care
    D. Cutting income taxes

10. One way of differentiating between ideologies is their view of tradition. Which of the following ideologies is not hostile to tradition?

A. Anarchism
B. American conservatism
C. Classical liberalism
D. Socialism

ANSWERS

1. An ideology is set of beliefs that reflect a person's outlook on the world. Ideologies are important because they shape how we perceive and interact with the world. In politics, they affect the voting choices we make and the policies we support.

2. Fundamentalism is the belief that a religious text is absolutely, literally true. This ideology also states that anything that opposes the text must be wrong. All behavior and belief must be guided by this central text, and anything else is sinful.

3. The core elements of classical liberalism include the importance of freedom, political equality, limited government, the free market, and a faith in reason and progress.

4. Traditional conservatism was hostile to the spread of democracy and the free market because they undermined tradition. American conservatism embraces both of these ideas.

5. Socialists argue that although liberalism promises freedom and equality, it does not deliver them because of the inequalities of the market. Therefore, socialists want the government to play a very strong role in the economy—perhaps even controlling it entirely—in order to rectify the failings of liberalism.

6. B

7. C

8. A

9. D

10. B

Suggested Reading

- Bakunin, Mikhail. *Statism and Anarchy*. New York: Cambridge University Press, 1990.

The classic statement of anarchism.

- Burke, Edmund. *Reflections on the Revolution in France*. Indianapolis: Hackett, 1987.

A prominent exposition of classical conservatism.

- Dahl, Robert. *Polyarchy*. New Haven, Conn.: Yale University Press, 1972.

A recent examination of democratic theory, although Dahl's polyarchy is not quite the same as democracy.

- Fukuyama, Francis. *The End of History and the Last Man*. New York: Free Press, 1992.

A foundational philosophical text of the contemporary neoconservative movement in the United States.

- Hayek, F. A. *The Road to Serfdom*. Chicago: University of Chicago Press, 1994.

A recent exposition of free market conservatism.

- Nozick, Robert. *Anarchy, State and Utopia*. New York: Basic Books, 1977.

A philosophically rich defense of libertarian views.

- Smith, Adam. *The Wealth of Nations.* New York: Modern Library, 1994.

The first formulation of the key ideas of free market capitalism. An immensely influential book.

Useful Websites

- www.americanprogress.org

The website of the Center for American Progress, an American liberal organization.

- www.balancedpolitics.org/ideology.htm

This website gives side-by-side comparisons of American liberalism and conservatism.

- www.cato.org

The website of the Cato Institute, a leading libertarian think tank.

- www.conservative.org

The website of the American Conservative Union, which promotes conservatism and rates politicians.

- www.lp.org

The website of the American Libertarian Party.

- www.typology.people-press.org

This website contains a thorough discussion of the "Red State/ Blue State" divide in the United States.

NATIONS AND STATES

Overview

Like an ideology, our nationality frequently determines how we behave and how we view politics. In the United States, many people think of themselves as "proud Americans." They might display flags in their yards or on their cars, or they might wear flag lapel pins. They might display yellow ribbons as a sign of support for American troops around the globe. Particularly since the terrorist attacks of September 11, 2001, many Americans have felt strongly patriotic.

For much of the last 500 years, the nation-state has been the dominant political unit. But nation-states did not always exist. Indeed, other political forms dominated the world for most of world history, and the nation-state is a relatively recent phenomenon. Today, the nation-state still predominates, even as the recent rise of globalization and devolution promises to fundamentally alter global politics.

Key Terms

In this section, we cover three of the most important terms in political science:

1. **Nation:** a large group of people linked by a similar culture, language, and history

2. **State:** a political unit that has sovereignty over a particular piece of land

3. **Nation-state:** a state that rules over a single nation

Because the nation-state dominates so much political discourse, many political scientists specialize in understanding how nation-states work internally, as well as how they relate to one another.

NATIONS

A **nation** is a large group of people who are linked by a similar culture, language, and history. Members of some nations share an ethnicity (almost everyone in South Korea is Korean, for example), whereas other nations consist of ethnically diverse groups of people (the United Kingdom, the United States, Australia, and Singapore, for instance). However, the members of a nation see themselves as connected. Fellow members are often regarded as part of an extended family. Many members of a nation take pride in being a part of something bigger than themselves as individuals, and they celebrate their nation.

> *EXAMPLE:* In common speech, we use the term *nation* to describe a collection of people with something in common. For example, some people refer to the "Red Sox Nation," consisting of all those who root for the Boston Red Sox. The term is used even more often as a synonym for country, which is technically incorrect.

People disagree about what counts as a nation. Nationhood sometimes transcends geographical boundaries. Some groups consider themselves to be nations, even though much of the world does not consider them that way. Kurds, for example, live in Turkey, Iraq, and Iran, but many Kurds believe they belong to a Kurdish nation. Also, members of a nation frequently differ in a variety of ways, including speaking different languages and participating in different cultural practices.

CHAPTER 3

EXAMPLE: Native American tribes in the United States are often referred to as nations because members of a particular tribe share a common set of language, history, and culture that differs from that of other Native American tribes. The language, history, and culture of the Cherokee Nation, for example, differs greatly from that of the Sioux Nation, which is different from that of the Iroquois Nation. Although the United States government grants these tribes some political autonomy (in other words, they can make many of their own laws), their classification as distinct nations comes from their shared ancestry and has nothing to do with their legal or political status.

In the end, determining what constitutes a nation is somewhat subjective. People may identify themselves as members of myriad nations, but even those identifications may change over time. And the strength of the identification also varies. The division between an ethnic group and a nation is a tricky one to make. To put it crudely, the moment that an ethnic group starts to view itself as a nation, it becomes a nation. The Kurdish people, for example, became a nation when they started thinking of themselves as an ethnic group with a common language, history, and culture that set them apart from the neighboring Turks, Arabs, and Persians.

EXAMPLE: Nations and their attendant nationalism in many ways caused World War I. In the decades leading up to the war, several European nations struggled to assert themselves on the global stage. These conflicts ratcheted up the tension. The event that directly precipitated the war—the assassination of Austrian archduke Franz Ferdinand in 1914—was also the result of nationalism: The assassin was a Serbian nationalist trying to free his nation from Austrian control.

Changing Identities

A good example of how membership in a nation changes over time comes from the history of the United States. In the early decades of the Republic, many Americans valued their connection to their home states over an attachment to the federal government. People identified with and felt loyal toward Virginia or Massachusetts rather than with the young United States. This reluctance to identify with other Americans contributed to the Civil War. After World War II, Americans closely identified with the United States as a single nation of one people. But in recent years, the "red-state/blue-state" divide has caused some people to increasingly identify with "their America," as opposed to the nation as a whole.

CHAPTER 3

STATES

A **state** is a political unit that has sovereignty over a particular piece of land. **Sovereignty** is the ultimate power within a territory. So the state has the power to make laws, defend its borders, and enact policies. The state also exercises a monopoly on the legitimate use of force: No group within its borders can use force legally without the permission of the state. In the United States, we use the word *state* to mean something more akin to the word *province* (the difference being that American states have more political autonomy and power than provinces in most other countries). But political scientists use the word *state* as a synonym for *sovereign governments.*

> ## Who is Sovereign
>
> A state is the ultimate authority within a territory. Smaller political units—such as city governments—exist within a state, but ultimately the supreme power rests with the state. The governments of the city of Chicago, for example, or Orange County, California, have some power to enforce rules within their territories. However, these governments do not have the final say: Local governments are not sovereign because they are subordinate to the federal government of the United States and must abide by the government's rules.

NATION-STATES

Political scientists use the term **nation-state** to refer to modern countries and their political apparatuses. A nation-state is a *state* that rules over a single *nation*. France, for example, is a nation-state, as is Japan. The people in both countries overwhelmingly share a common language, history, and culture. The term *nation-state* reflects the situation in which the boundaries of a state coincide with the geographical area occupied by a nation. There are also states that are not nations—such as Switzerland, whose citizens speak four different languages and have varied cultures. And there are nations that are not states, such as Kurdistan, a region in the Middle East lacking firm borders that is occupied by Kurds, but it is not considered to be an independent state by its neighboring nations of Syria and Turkey.

One sign of the nation-state's prevalence in global politics is that nearly all states refer to themselves as nation-states, regardless of their national makeup. Every government works to build a sense of national identity among its citizens, and sometimes governments even carefully create or craft that identity. For this reason, some scholars argue that the concepts of "nation" and "nation-state" are more about perception and feelings of identity than concrete facts. Most nation-states have citizens of more than one nationality. For example, the small groups of Catalonians in Spain, Bretons in France, and Ainu in Japan differ in nationality from the majority of people in those nation-states. Usually, the minority groups are very small.

Nation-State Minorities

Often, people in the dominant nationality within a nation-state will mistreat those in the minority. For many years, the government of Australia, dominated by the ancestors of European settlers, enacted many harsh policies against the indigenous Australians, known as the Aborigines. These policies included taking over Aboriginal land and removing indigenous children from their families and placing them in special schools for socialization.

Nation-Building

In many nation-states, the government actively promotes the idea of common nationality. Children learn the same language and history in state-sponsored schools, and public events frequently invoke cultural heroes and icons. Citizens are often encouraged to work for the betterment of the nation. These practices, among others, are known collectively as **nation-building.**

Foreign governments also participate in nation-building. Sometimes a government will give money and advice to another country to help nation-building. At other times, a country will engage in nation-building after it militarily occupies another country. Before leaving, the occupying power seeks to build a nation that can govern itself. In the early years of the twenty-first century, the United States intervened militarily and participated in nation-building in Afghanistan and Iraq.

Nefarious Nation-Building

At times, nation-building has been undertaken using nefarious means. Nazi Germany, for example, sought to unite its people through a shared hatred of common enemies, most notably the Jews. The government of the former Soviet Union promoted national identity by forcing very different ethnic groups to learn the same language, going so far as to outlaw the use of some local languages.

Nation-States Around the World

Today, most of Europe consists of nation-states. But in Africa and the Middle East, states frequently do not coincide with nations, largely as a result of European colonialism. In the nineteenth century, during what is now known as "the Scramble for Africa," the Europeans divided up the continent without regard to indigenous national boundaries. When the Europeans left and the former colonies became independent states, they mostly kept the borders established by the Europeans.

> *EXAMPLE:* In 1947, the British government withdrew from what was then known as Palestine. Shortly thereafter, the United Nations established the state of Israel, unevenly splitting the land between the Jews and the Arabs and giving the state of Israel sovereign domain over such Palestinian areas as the West Bank and the Gaza Strip. The resulting tensions and violence among Jews, Arabs, and Palestinians continue to this day.

Colonial Boundaries

According to legend, the English set the boundaries of the Gambia, a small country in West Africa, by firing a cannon from a ship on the Gambia River and then marking that nation's boundary according to where the cannonballs fell.

The Struggle for the Nation-State

Throughout modern history, many groups have worked very hard to create nation-states. Sometimes, these efforts succeed, as with the unification of Italy in the late nineteenth century; the dissolution of the Austro-Hungarian Empire after World War I into the discrete nation-states of Austria, Czechoslovakia, Hungary, Poland, and Yugoslavia; and the independence of Eritrea from Ethiopia in the late twentieth century. In some cases, however, people have failed thus far in their attempts to create a distinct nation-state. Groups that continue to agitate for a nation-state include the Basques in Spain, as well as the Palestinians and the Kurds in the Middle East.

Empire

An **empire** is a state that governs more than one national group, usually as a result of conquest. One national group frequently dominates, giving members of that group a special place in the regime. Empires have existed in every era of human history, from the ancient empires of Egypt, China, Ghana, and Rome to the modern British Empire.

The Rise of the Nation-State

The nation-state developed fairly recently. Prior to the 1500s, in Europe, the nation-state as we know it did not exist. Back then, most people did not consider themselves part of a nation; they rarely left their village and knew little of the larger world. If anything, people were more likely to identify themselves with their region or local lord. At the same time, the rulers of states frequently had little control over their countries. Instead, local feudal lords had a great deal of power, and kings often had to depend on the goodwill of their subordinates to rule. Laws and practices varied a great deal from one part of the country to another. The timeline on page 65 explains some key events that led to the rise of the nation-state.

In the early modern era, a number of monarchs began to consolidate power by weakening the feudal nobles and allying themselves with the emerging commercial classes. This difficult process sometimes required violence. The consolidation of power also took a long time. Kings and queens worked to bring all the people of their territories under unified rule. Not surprisingly, then, the birth of the nation-state also saw the first rumblings of nationalism, as monarchs encouraged their subjects to feel loyalty toward the newly established nations. The modern, integrated nation-state became clearly established in most of Europe during the nineteenth century.

EXAMPLE: Russia is a great example of consolidation of power by monarchs. Throughout most of the medieval era, what became Russia was a minor principality centered on the city of Moscow. Over the course of a few hundred years, the rulers of Moscow took over more land, eventually expanding to cover much of what is now Russia. This expansion came through a mix of diplomacy and war. When Ivan IV—also known as Ivan the Terrible—came of age and assumed the throne in 1547, he was crowned the first czar. He proceeded to devastate the nobility by means of a secret police and gained the loyalty of commercial classes by giving them positions in a new state bureaucracy. These actions led to the deaths of thousands.

THE RISE OF THE EUROPEAN NATION-STATE	
Time Frame	**Major Event**
Pre-1500s	Most people lived in small villages; they paid tithes to feudal landlords, didn't travel, and cared little for anything beyond the village.
1485	Henry VII wins the War of the Roses in England, begins the Tudor dynasty, and starts the development of the English nation-state.
1492	Spanish monarchs Ferdinand and Isabella finish taking back all of Spain from the Muslims; the era of Spain as a global power begins.
1547–1584	Ivan the Terrible rules Russia; he unifies the government and creates the first Russian nation-state.
1638–1715	Louis XIV of France creates an absolute monarchy; France emerges as the dominant power in Europe.
1648	Peace of Westphalia cements the legal status of the nation-state as sovereign.
1789	The French Revolution begins; it creates the modern French nation-state and sparks nationalism around Europe.
1871	Unification of Italy and Germany is complete.
1919	Treaty of Versailles ends World War I; it breaks up several multinational empires and creates many new nation-states.
1945	The United Nations forms.

CHAPTER 3

The Catholic Church and the Rise of the Nation-State

Newly emerging nation-states in the sixteenth and seventeenth centuries had a complex relationship with the predominant transnational power of the time, the Catholic Church. At times, partial nation-states were useful tools for the Catholic Church. On several occasions, for example, France and Spain intervened in Italy at the invitation of the Pope. But some monarchs wanted control over their national churches in order to get absolute power. In England, the dispute over who controlled the English church led Henry VIII to break from the Pope and establish an independent Protestant church in the 1530s. This break with the Catholic Church gave the English something to rally around, thus encouraging them to develop loyalty toward the English nation-state. At the same time, some devout Catholics in England refused to convert; their displeasure ultimately led to repression and civil war.

THE THIRTY YEARS' WAR AND THE PEACE OF WESTPHALIA

The Thirty Years' War, fought throughout central Europe from 1618–1648 between Protestants and Catholics, laid the legal foundation for the nation-state. The war involved many nations of Europe, including many small German states, the Austrian Empire, Sweden, France, and Spain. Despite a brutal war, the Catholics were unable to overturn Protestantism. The treaty that ended the war, called the Peace of Westphalia, decreed that the sovereign ruler of a state had power over all elements of both the nation and the state, including religion. Thus, the modern idea of a sovereign state was born.

CENTRALIZATION

Centralization, or the process by which law- and policymaking become centrally located, helped spur the development of nation-states. Final power rested with the central government, which made the laws and practices more uniform across the country. A single centralized authority, rather than many diverse local authorities, allowed nation-states to quickly develop their economies. Merchants could trade throughout the nation without worrying about local taxes and regulations. Also, the nation-state was much stronger militarily than the feudal state. Rulers were able to create national armies, which were not dependent on the nobility. The armies could receive consistent training so that all units could work well together. In many cases, the newly emerging nation-states dominated the older forms of political organization.

EXAMPLE: In the eighteenth century, nobles held most of the power in Poland. The monarch was very weak. As a result, Poland could not defeat its powerful neighbors Austria, Prussia, and Russia. These three centralized nation-states partitioned Poland on three different occasions—1772, 1793, and 1795—eventually eliminating Poland until 1918, when a new Republic of Poland formed.

CHAPTER 3

The Importance of Napoleon

Napoleon Bonaparte was a key figure in the development of the nation-state. Amid the chaos of the French Revolution in the late eighteenth century, most remaining medieval and feudal laws were overturned and a truly national law code was established. Similarly, a national military was created. Although not the only reason, France's status as a nation-state was a key factor in its ability to dominate feudal neighbors in Italy and Germany. Napoleon's military victories also paved the way for the emergence of nation-states in the rest of Europe: In many places, the people rallied together as a nation in order to defeat Napoleon.

Constitutions and the Structure of Government

Every country has a constitution of some sort that outlines the government's structure. A **constitution** is simply the set of rules that govern how power is distributed and exercised. In other words, these rules structure the government of a state. Without such a set of rules, the state could not function and anarchy would reign. Although no constitution can cover every possible question or issue, all states need to spell out at least the fundamental matters of the distribution and use of power.

WRITTEN AND UNWRITTEN CONSTITUTIONS

Some constitutions—such as that of the United States or the Basic Law of Germany—are codified into written documents. In other states, such as the United Kingdom, the constitution consists of many documents, laws, court rulings, and traditional practices that have never been compiled into a single document. But in every case, custom, history, and tradition play an important role.

> ### Unwritten Rules of the United States
>
> Although the U.S. Constitution is a written document, many of the keys to the American political system are not in it. Perhaps the best example is the power of judicial review—the authority to decide if a law is constitutional. The Supreme Court gave itself this power in the case of *Marbury v. Madison* (1803). Similarly, the role of political parties developed over time—and does not appear in the Constitution.

CONSTITUTIONAL DESIGN

Strong constitutions share three characteristics, or principles, of constitution design:

1. **Attentive to tradition:** People prefer rules that resemble past rules. They are unlikely to follow a new set of rules if it differs widely from what they are used to doing. This principle holds particularly true for customs that have existed for a long time.

2. **Open to change:** A constitution should be amendable. Although it should not be too easy to change, making a constitution too rigid may straitjacket future leaders, who may deal with dramatically different circumstances.

   > **EXAMPLE:** The U.S. Constitution has been amended nearly thirty times, allowing Americans to adapt their structure of government to changing mores, beliefs, and practices. The Bill of Rights was the first set of amendments. Other amendments include the Thirteenth Amendment, which made slavery illegal in 1865, and the Nineteenth Amendment, which gave women the right to vote in 1920.

3. **A harness to personal ambition:** In a good government, the leaders have a strong incentive to prioritize the country over personal ambition. A good, strong constitution creates a situation in which the leaders' ambition leads them to work for the public good, not for personal gain. Without such incentives, rulers, elected or otherwise, may very well ignore the public good.

Although these three principles of constitutional design help ensure solid governmental structures, ultimately they are merely guidelines. Some successful constitutions do not include them, and a number of states have succeeded in imposing governments that differ greatly from tradition. Unfortunately, any radical departures from tradition or history usually require violence.

> *EXAMPLE:* After a fourteen-year war to gain independence from Portugal, Angola entered into a decades-long civil war to determine which ethnic political party would head the country. Intervention from other nation-states, which favored one party over another and wanted to see their favorite gain dominance, exacerbated the violence.

Length of Constitutions

Some constitutions are short documents. The U.S. Constitution, for example, covers only a few pages. Others are lengthy. The Basic Law of Germany, for example, is roughly five times as long as the U.S. Constitution. As a general rule, older constitutions are shorter than newer constitutions.

> *EXAMPLE:* In the United States, state constitutions are frequently far longer than the federal one, which was ratified in 1789. In part, this is because most state constitutions were written after the federal one. Even states that predate the federal Constitution have rewritten their constitutions, sometimes more than once.

The Longest Constitution

According to some estimates, the state of Alabama has the world's longest constitution, with approximately 740 amendments.

The Advantages of Vagueness

Constitutions, particularly short ones, tend to be vague in their contents. Vague constitutions have two advantages:

1. **They easily adapt to changing circumstances.** Social and political circumstances sometimes change very rapidly, and an excessively specific constitution can create problems if a new political era dawns.

2. **They foster cooperation.** Vague constitutions encourage political leaders to work together to determine the specific policies through negotiation.

> *EXAMPLE:* The vague U.S. Constitution has encouraged political leaders to work together through congressional committees. These committees have become a hallmark of the American democratic process.

Systems of Government

A **system of government** distributes power among different parts and levels of the state. Political scientists study the uses of power, including how power is distributed within a state. The amount of power held by the central government determines the system of government a state has. There are three main systems of government used today: unitary systems, federal systems, and confederate systems.

CHAPTER 3

THREE SYSTEMS OF GOVERNMENT			
System	Level of Central-ization	Strength	Weakness
Unitary (e.g., China, France, Japan, United Kingdom)	High	Sets uniform policies that direct the entire nation	Disregards local differences
Federal (e.g., United States, Germany, Australia, Canada)	Medium	Gives local governments more power	Sacrifices national uniformity on some issues
Confederate (e.g., Confederate States of America, Belgium)	Low	Gives local/ regional governments almost complete control	Sets no significant uniform national policies

UNITARY SYSTEMS

A **unitary system** has the highest degree of centralization. In a unitary state, the central government holds all the power. Lower-level governments, if they exist at all, do nothing but implement the policies of the national government. In a purely unitary state, the same set of laws applies throughout the nation, without variation. Unitary states create national policy, which is then applied uniformly. This uniformity sometimes serves as an advantage because people and businesses know exactly what to expect from the laws, regardless of geographical location. At the same time, to maintain its uniformity, a unitary government must overlook local differences that might call for different rules or policies.

EXAMPLE: Most absolute monarchies and tyrannies operate under unitary systems. But democratic unitary states exist as well. In France, for example, the central government makes virtually all of the decisions.

FEDERAL SYSTEMS

A **federal system** has a mix of national and state or local governments. The federal government usually trumps local governments in matters of defense and foreign policy, but local governments have a great deal of say over most other policy areas. Sometimes local governments administer national policies, which means that, in practice, the "national" policy varies a great deal from place to place.

EXAMPLE: In the United States, state governments administered Aid to Families with Dependent Children (AFDC) throughout the length of the program, 1935–1997. Although the federal government set certain rules for how the money was to be spent, state governments had the power to administer it as they saw fit. Some states, therefore, gave little money through AFDC, whereas others were much more generous.

Often, the boundary between national and local power is blurred. Federal systems have the opposite strengths and weaknesses of unitary systems: They excel at factoring in local circumstances but often fail to have a coherent national policy.

EXAMPLE: The United States, Mexico, and Canada operate under federal systems. These states have a mix of national and state governments that share power and policymaking responsibilities.

CHAPTER 3

CONFEDERATE SYSTEMS

A confederate system sits at the other extreme in terms of centralization. A confederacy is a loose relationship among a number of smaller political units. The vast majority of political power rests with the local governments; the central federal government has very little power. Local governments have a great deal of freedom to act as they wish, but this freedom often leads to conflicts between states and the federal government. In some cases, a confederacy is little more than an alliance between independent states.

EXAMPLE: For Americans, the Confederate States of America—which governed the South during the Civil War—is the best-known example of a confederacy, but there have been others. In fact, the first government of the United States, created by the Articles of Confederation (finished in 1777), was this type of system. Today, Belgium is basically a confederacy between two largely independent states, Flanders in the north and Wallonia in the south.

The Future of Nation-States

Although the nation-state has been the predominant unit of political organization for most of the last few centuries, its future is uncertain. Two trends point to the nation-state as receding in importance, but these trends sometimes contradict each other. Still, globalization and devolution continue to occur at a rapid rate throughout the twenty-first-century world, and both will affect the future of nation-states.

GLOBALIZATION

The first major trend is **globalization.** Over the last few decades, national boundaries have broken down in a variety of ways, including economically. In today's truly global economy, money and goods travel across borders in huge quantities and at great speed. Many corporations build parts in a variety of countries, then assemble them in yet another country. Most goods are no longer "made in America," for example, because much of the manufacturing often happens in other places, whereas final assembly occurs in the United States. The rapid growth of international investing has further globalized the economy. Globalization often leads to transnationalism, so should this globalizing trend continue, the nation-state might give way to the transnational government.

The Perils of Globalization

Since the mid-1990s, people from around the world have attacked globalization. Environmentalists see globalization as a disaster for the environment, labor unions fear for their members' jobs in a global marketplace, and others see globalization itself as a cause of poverty in developing countries. Most governments continue to favor globalization, but antiglobalization protesters have made their mark by demonstrating against meetings of the World Bank, the International Monetary Fund, and other international economic institutions. During the so-called Battle of Seattle in 1999, thousands of protesters swarmed the hotel and convention centers at which meetings of the World Trade Organization were being held.

Transnationalism

Transnationalism has also occurred at the political level. International organizations, such as the United Nations and the World Trade Organization, play an ever-increasing role on the political stage, and nations join them for such benefits as military protection and economic security. In the case of the European Union, national boundaries have very little meaning. All citizens can travel, live, and work freely throughout the European Union, and all internal tariffs and trade restrictions have been abolished. Some residents see themselves as citizens of a new European Union nation, not of their smaller countries. Transnational governments and groups literally transcend geographical and political boundaries.

> *EXAMPLE:* The World Trade Organization, the United Nations, and the World Bank are just a few examples of international organizations that sometimes act like governments or play a substantial role in international relations. Other examples include the Organization of American States, the North Atlantic Treaty Organization, the Organization for Economic Cooperation and Development, and the Organization of Petroleum Exporting Countries.

The fact that increasing numbers of people around the world speak the same language demonstrates the transnational trend. English has become something of an international language, but other languages (such as French, Chinese, and Russian) are also spoken by many around the world. Overall, the total number of languages spoken is decreasing, while the total number of speakers of certain dominant languages is increasing.

DEVOLUTION

The second trend that marks the recession of nation-states concerns the increase in political power being given to local governments, sometimes to the point of autonomy. This trend is sometimes called **devolution** because states are said to devolve power back to local governments. In the United Kingdom, for example, Scotland has been granted a great deal of autonomy, as has Catalonia in Spain. Should this trend continue, local governments would replace national or central governments.

Sample Test Questions

1. What is a nation?

2. Describe the rise of the nation-state.

3. What two current trends raise doubts about the future of the nation-state?

4. Which definition best describes nation-building?

   A. The process of drawing new borders for countries
   B. The effort to build a sense of national identity among citizens
   C. Conquering a neighboring nation
   D. Giving sovereign power to a different group of people

5. Why has nation-building taken on increased prominence in recent years?

   A. Canadian efforts to overcome Québécois subnationalism
   B. The division in the United States between "red states" and "blue states"
   C. The rise of the European Union
   D. The American occupation of Afghanistan and Iraq

6. Which of the following is *not* a characteristic of a state?

   A. Motivated by profit
   B. Sovereign power
   C. Monopoly on the legitimate use of force
   D. The power to make laws for all citizens

7. What does a constitution represent?

    A. The history of a country and its government
    B. The power to control local governments
    C. The rules that determine the distribution and exercise
       of power
    D. A tradition that is pushed aside as times change

8. Why is it a bad idea to make a constitution too easy
    to change?

    A. It undermines the stability of the government.
    B. It assumes that the writers of the constitution were
       foolish.
    C. It shows disloyalty to the past
    D. We aren't as wise as our predecessors

9. Which of the following best describes a unitary state?

    A. It works closely with its neighbors.
    B. It devolves power to local jurisdictions.
    C. It concentrates all power in the central government.
    D. It does not hold elections.

10. What is transnationalism?

    A. The spread of loyalties to local identities
    B. The growth of nationalism
    C. The breakdown of national boundaries
    D. The end of the nation-state

ANSWERS

1. A nation is a group of people who share a common language, history, and culture.

2. The nation-state began to emerge in the early modern era. Monarchs worked to unify their nations by concentrating

power in the central government and undermining the power of the nobility. The process took a long time and frequently required violence.

3. Transnationalism, sometimes called globalization, is the rise of trade and political arrangements that break down national borders. Devolution is the practice of governments ceding power to regional government, sometimes even granting them autonomy.

4. B

5. D

6. A

7. C

8. A

9. C

10. C

CHAPTER 3

Suggested Reading

- Aristotle. *Politics*. Translated by C. D. C. Reeve. Indianapolis: Hackett, 1998.

This important work includes a detailed discussion of how constitutions are defined and explains what results different types of constitutions have.

- Bakvis, Herman, and William M. Chandler. *Federalism and the Role of the State*. Toronto: University of Toronto Press, 1987.

A study of the way federalism affects governing.

• Goldwin, Robert A., Art Kaufman, and William A. Scham-bra, eds. *Forging Unity Out of Diversity: The Approaches of Eight Nations.* Washington, D.C.: American Enterprise Institute, 1989.

A comparative analysis of how countries deal with ethnic and religious differences.

• Montesquieu, Baron de. *The Spirit of the Laws.* Translated by Ann M. Cohler, Basta C. Miller, and Harold Stone. New York: Cambridge University Press, 1989.

Montesquieu was one of the most influential theorists of laws and constitutions in the Western world.

• McDonald, Forrest. *E Pluribus Unum: The Formation of the American Republic, 1776-1790.* Indianapolis: Liberty Press, 1979.

A good account of the difficulties of writing a constitution in the United States. It also includes a history of the Articles of Confederation.

• Reich, Robert. *The Work of Nations.* Reprint, New York: Vintage, 1992.

Reich argues that national borders mean very little in the global economy and that nations need to adopt new ways of thinking about the international system.

• Riker, William. *Federalism: Origin, Operation, Significance.* Boston: Little, Brown, 1964.

A valuable account of federalism.

• Sunstein, Cass R. *Designing Democracy: What Constitutions Do.* New York: Oxford University Press, 2001.

A good account of the importance of sound constitutions in creating a democratic state.

Useful Websites

- www.access.gpo.gov/congress/senate/constitution/toc.html
Analysis and interpretation of the U.S. Constitution.

- http://archives.gov/historical-docs
Online facsimiles and information about some of the nation's most important historical documents, including the Declaration of Independence and the Louisiana Purchase.

- www.europa.eu
A useful and well-organized site with links to the many different parts of the institutions of the European Union.

- www.uni-wuerzburg.de/law/index.html
The website of the International Constitutional Law Project, which monitors the status of constitutions and amendments from all over the world.

CHAPTER 3

POLITICAL ECONOMY

4

Overview

Thinkers and politicians throughout the ages have discussed economic issues, but they usually subordinated a strong economy to other goals, such as a centralized government or the acquisition of more territory. Adam Smith's publication of *The Wealth of Nations* in 1776 brought economics into the modern era. Smith and later scholars focused on how the economy works best and most efficiently, but they did not consider what moral goals the economy should serve. Smith argued that the most efficient economy was a free-market economy, with little government interference. When Britain and other nations began to put Smith's theories into practice, their economies expanded rapidly and vast wealth was created. Even though economics has changed greatly since his time, it is fair to say that we live in Adam Smith's world.

Today all governments must work to implement sound economic policy. But there are no easy answers to economic issues. Often, different parts of society want different things, and what helps one part hurts another. And sometimes dealing with one problem causes another. In a democracy, politicians who fail to fix the economy—or even those who appear to be doing nothing to solve economic problems—face very angry voters. So politicians need to pay attention to economics.

Politics and money frequently intersect, and political scientists call that intersection **political economy.** The two realms interact and affect each other in complex ways, making it difficult to tell where one begins or ends. The state is expected to play a role in shaping the economy, so naturally the state affects and alters the economy. But the economy also affects the state: A state that cannot make the economy grow, or distribute it in a manner seen to be fair, could be in a great deal of trouble. And a booming economy can save even inept or corrupt leaders.

Rational Choice

As different academic fields, political science and economics utilize different research methods and techniques of analysis. The study of political economy brings together these diverse methods and techniques. One of the most prominent examples of this interdisciplinary blending is **rational choice theory.** Scholars use rational choice, a model derived from economics, to understand people and behavior. According to this view, humans act to maximize their outcomes—that is, to get the most benefit and profit from their actions. To this end, people make decisions rationally based on whatever information they can get. To put it crudely, people act in a selfish manner, using reason to get what they want.

Minimaxing

The rational choice approach is also sometimes called the **minimax approach,** a term that comes from the military. People act to minimize their maximum losses and to maximize their minimum gains.

Rational choice defines reason in a very specific way: Humans use reason to get what they want. But this is not the only way of defining the term, and this definition of reason applies only to a narrow range of study and behavior. Economists and political scientists do not assume that people always act this way. Rational choice only looks at certain types of human behavior and decision-making, but this model has become very influential in political science. The rational choice approach has been adopted to explain a great variety of behaviors—from how members of Congress act in their home districts to how individuals decide to join (or not join) interest groups.

CHAPTER 4

Types of Economies

An economy is a system whereby goods are produced and ex-
changed. Without a viable economy, a state will collapse. There
are three main types of economies: free market, command, and
mixed. The chart below compares free-market and command
economies; mixed economies are a combination of the two.

FREE-MARKET VERSUS COMMAND ECONOMIES	
Free-Market Economies	**Command Economies**
Usually occur in democratic states	Usually occur in communist or authoritarian states
Individuals and businesses make their own economic decisions.	The state's central government makes all of the country's economic decisions.

FREE-MARKET ECONOMIES

In **free-market economies,** which are essentially capitalist
economies, businesses and individuals have the freedom to pursue their own economic interests, buying and selling goods on
a competitive market, which naturally determines a fair price
for goods and services.

COMMAND ECONOMIES

A **command economy** is also known as a **centrally planned
economy** because the central, or national, government plans
the economy. Generally, communist states have command
economies, although China has been moving recently toward
a capitalist economy. In a communist society, the central government controls the entire economy, allocating resources and
dictating prices for goods and services. Some noncommunist
authoritarian states also have command economies. In times
of war, most states—even democratic, free-market states—take
an active role in economic planning but not necessarily to the
extent of communist states.

EXAMPLE: During World War II, the United States largely took control of the American economy, forcing businesses to build tanks, planes, and ammunition instead of normal consumer goods. Supplies were also rationed. For example, to buy more toothpaste, people were obliged to return the empty tube because metal was in short supply.

Inefficiencies of Command Economies

Command economies are often very inefficient because these economies try to ignore the laws of supply and demand. In most cases, a black market arises to fill the demands overlooked by the central plan. Economic growth overall is often slower than in states with free markets. Some command economies claim to act to promote economic equality, but often the elites in the government live far better than others.

The Triumph of Capitalism

Although command economies were once considered viable alternatives to free-market capitalist economies, poor economic performance in countries with planned economies proved that capitalism was much more efficient. The former Soviet Union's centrally planned economy performed so poorly, for example, that the government literally collapsed in 1990–1991. North Korea's command economy also failed completely more than a decade ago, causing rampant starvation, which has been alleviated only by international food donations. Chinese leaders, in contrast, recognized more than twenty years ago that the centrally planned economy could not meet their nation's needs, which is why they have privatized agricultural production and many other industries. China has since legalized the ownership of private property and courted massive amounts in foreign investments, despite the fact that the state remains severely authoritarian.

MIXED ECONOMIES

A **mixed economy** combines elements of free-market and command economies. Even among free-market states, the government usually takes some action to direct the economy. These moves are made for a variety of reasons; for example, some are designed to protect certain industries or help consumers. In economic language, this means that most states have mixed economies.

> *EXAMPLE:* Agricultural subsidies, which exist in many countries (including the United States), are a common way governments intervene in the economy. In some cases, these policies are designed to keep food prices low without bankrupting farmers. In other cases, they work to protect domestic agriculture. Even the price of milk is strongly influenced by government policy in the United States.

Economic Problems

Every government struggles with unemployment, inflation, and recession/depression, and each government must enact policies to combat these problems. In the United States, both unemployment and inflation have been fairly low (5 percent or lower) for much of the past two decades. But even low unemployment and inflation affect and undermine economic growth. The following chart summarizes the economic problems faced by states.

STATES' ECONOMIC PROBLEMS		
Unemployment	**Inflation**	**Recession/Depression**
Not everyone who wants to work has a job.	The price of goods increases.	Economic failure or collapse occurs in many sectors of the economy.

UNEMPLOYMENT

Unemployment occurs when there simply are not enough jobs for everyone who wishes to have one. Every economy has some unemployment because people leave jobs (by choice or against their will) and are usually unemployed for a time before they find new employment. Others are unemployed for longer periods.

EXAMPLE: Analysts measure unemployment as a percentage of the work force who cannot find jobs. What counts as high or low unemployment is, to some extent, relative. In the United States, analysts consider a rate of unemployment above 5-6 percent to be high, even though many western European countries frequently have unemployment rates above 10 percent.

Measuring Unemployment

Analysts have difficulty measuring unemployment because polling every eligible person to find out whether he or she has a job is impossible. Therefore, analysts rely on other methods to measure unemployment. In the United States, the official jobless (or unemployment) rate is based on the number of people claiming unemployment benefits. But not all jobless people file for unemployment benefits, and people whose benefits have expired are not counted, so even this method has potential flaws.

Underemployment

Underemployment, a condition related to unemployment, occurs when a person does not work full time or does not use all of his or her skills (as when a person with a PhD in biology waits tables in a restaurant). The underemployment rate sometimes indicates more about the state of the economy than unemployment because many people want full-time work but cannot find it and thus might take whatever part-time jobs they can. Some analysts see underemployment as being better than unemployment because the underemployed are not as prone to poverty as the unemployed. In reality, underemployed people usually do not qualify for unemployment benefits, so the underemployed may be worse off than those without jobs.

Why Be Unemployed?

The rational choice approach helps political scientists understand why some people will stay unemployed rather than take part-time work. This decision seems irrational because any job is better than no job. But in many cases, it makes financial sense to stay unemployed: The unemployment benefits might be higher than the wages from a part-time job. Similarly, those without jobs often qualify for programs, such as free or cheaper health care, that are unavailable to the underemployed. Sometimes it makes sense for people to choose to stay unemployed.

Dangers of Unemployment

Unemployment is a problem because it means that some people in society are not making any money, which puts them in grave danger of tremendous poverty or worse. When unemployment rises to high levels, those without jobs may become hostile to the government, blaming it and their leaders for their situation. At such times, political shakiness or insecurity can result.

In extreme cases, governments have fallen due to their high rates of unemployment.

EXAMPLE: During the Great Depression, unemployment was extremely high around the world—approaching 30 percent in some places. The large number of jobless people created tremendous instability in many countries, including Germany. There the high unemployment, along with hyperinflation, contributed to the rise of Nazism. The middle class was financially wiped out, and many citizens began to blame the new democratic government and saw the Nazi Party as a positive regime change.

Unemployment rates vary from place to place within a country. In the early years of the twenty-first century, for example, unemployment in Washington State was higher than in most other places in the United States because the Seattle-area economy is heavily dependent on high-tech industries, which underwent a serious slump around this time. Likewise, the closing of a factory can devastate the local economy even if the rest of the nation's economy is strong.

INFLATION

Inflation occurs when the prices of goods and services begin to rise. Analysts measure inflation as a percentage increase in price over the course of a year. So, if inflation is 10 percent, an item that costs $1 will cost $1.10 a year later. The official inflation rate is an average of price increases for all goods and services, so it may not apply exactly to any one given good.

Inflation also means that the currency becomes worth less. In the above example, one dollar is now worth less than it once was. Economists refer to this decrease as a decline in **buying power,** which is the amount of goods and services money can buy. In other words, if a person's salary stays the same but inflation occurs, her buying power will go down. This person will be poorer because she can no longer afford the things she used to buy as the price of those goods increases.

EXAMPLE: According to the Bureau of Labor Statistics, $1 from 1986 had the buying power of $1.86 in 2006. In other words, if a hamburger cost you $1 in 1986, you'd have to pay $1.86 for it today. This difference of $0.86 many not seem significant until you start purchasing more expensive items. A car that cost you $10,000 in 1986 would cost you more than $18,000 today, and a $100,000 home in 1986 would now cost you more than $180,000.

CHAPTER 4

Excess Demand

In general, the basic law of supply and demand causes inflation. When the demand for something exceeds supply (what economists call **excess demand**), the price goes up. Excess demand and high inflation have a variety of causes:

- A bad harvest

- Shortages due to war

- A natural disaster

- Increased consumer desire (that is, more people wanting a particular good)

- Increased consumer spending power

Other factors contribute to inflation too, such as when a company intentionally underproduces an item to drive up prices or when a government steps in to increase or decrease inflation. We cover the economic policies of governments later in the chapter, particularly in the sections on fiscal policy.

Dangers of Inflation

High inflation (defined as more than 5 percent in North America and Europe) can do the following:

- Create economic turbulence

- Exaggerate a person's financial success or failure so that he becomes rich or poor very quickly

- Increase the number of people who are at risk for poverty (if things cost more, then more people may be considered poor)

- Cause political instability (historically, many authoritarian regimes have risen to power during periods of extremely high inflation)

Inflation Around the Globe

In the industrialized world, inflation has remained low since 1990. But severe inflation—called *hyperinflation*—does happen sometimes. In 1994, for example, inflation in Brazil was more than 3,000 percent. In the 1930s in some European countries, inflation was similarly high, and stories were told about people hauling money in a wheelbarrow to the store in order to pay for a single loaf of bread.

Balancing Unemployment and Inflation

All governments must balance the effects of unemployment with those of inflation. In most cases, reducing unemployment usually requires spending more money, which causes prices to increase. Similarly, reducing inflation often means reducing the amount of money spent, which usually increases unemployment. Balancing these goals is a difficult but necessary governmental task.

RECESSION AND DEPRESSION

All governments want to avoid an economic **recession,** which is a period of decline in the economy. Recessions often are accompanied by high unemployment and, sometimes, high inflation. Even worse is a **depression,** an economic downturn that dips deeper and lasts longer than a recession.

EXAMPLE: When the stock market crashed on October 24, 1929, the world fell into the Great Depression, one of the most severe economic downturns of the industrial era. Unemployment skyrocketed, reaching about 33 percent in the United States. Many people suffered from dire poverty, and some starved. The depression did not fully end in the United States until the nation entered World War II at the end of 1941.

Economic Growth

Perhaps the most obvious economic goal for a nation-state is **economic growth,** or an increase in the total value of the country's economy. Nation-states strive for economic growth to increase the standard of living for their citizens and to gain more power in the world market. When growth is slow or when the economy actually shrinks in size, leaders often face strong criticism and greater opposition.

The 1992 Presidential Election

The economy took center stage in the 1992 presidential election. Incumbent George H. W. Bush enjoyed tremendous popularity after the successful Persian Gulf War, but his popularity plummeted as people began to worry about the economy. Bush's Democratic opponent, Bill Clinton, focused heavily on the economy in his campaign stumping. In fact, a sign prominently displayed in Clinton's campaign headquarters read, "It's the Economy, Stupid." The American perception of a bad economy was one factor that doomed Bush's chance for reelection.

GROSS DOMESTIC PRODUCT

Gross domestic product (GDP) is the measure of the total amount of all economic transactions within a state. An increase in GDP leads to economic growth. Because economic growth means that the country as a whole is richer, it makes sense that a government will seek to increase the nation's GDP.

GDP is frequently measured *per capita,* as the amount of GDP for each person. To calculate per capita GDP, divide the total GDP by the number of people in the country. Countries have widely different population sizes, so comparing their GDPs is not all that helpful. Economists and political scientists do, however, compare per capita GDP to get an idea of the relative wealth or poverty among different countries.

Per capita GDP varies widely around the world. The following table shows some examples of global GDP. As the table illustrates, in industrialized countries, per capita GDP can be more than $30,000 a year, but in very poor countries, per capita GDP is sometimes less than $1,000.

GDPs AROUND THE WORLD IN 2006	
Nation	**GDP per Capita (approximate)**
United States	$42,000
United Kingdom	$31,000
Germany	$30,000
Israel	$22,000
Mexico	$10,000
Iran	$8,000
China	$6,000
El Salvador	$5,000
Vietnam	$3,000
Nigeria	$1,000
Malawi	$600

INCOME DISTRIBUTION

Another sign of economic growth relates to **income distribution,** or how the wealth of a country is divided up. In most societies, in the present as well as in the past, just a few people possess great wealth, whereas most people are poor. Many modern democracies work to distribute wealth more equally through a variety of means, including welfare. But even in some democracies, including the United States, the richest people have far more money than the poorest.

Equity

Equity occurs when an economic transaction is fair to all those involved. Although not the same as equal income distribution, equity is an important part of a fair economy.

Most governments have laws and policies designed to ensure equity. Without such policies, many people would not engage in economic activity.

Measuring Income Distribution

Measuring income distribution is difficult. Simply measuring the average (mean) income can be misleading because extremes on either end skew the results. Nevertheless, analysts measure the median income to get a more accurate assessment of how the typical citizen fares because exactly one-half of people are below the median and one-half are above. Another way to measure income distribution is to examine wealth in quintiles (groups of 20 percent). For example, analysts might compare the amount of money owned by the richest 20 percent of the population with the amount of money owned by the poorest 20 percent.

Economic Inequality

Scholars hotly debate how much economic inequality is desirable. Some argue that a competitive economic market by necessity brings inequality, and thus some inequality among people is normal and natural. Giving hard workers and creative entrepreneurs more money than other people gives everyone the incentive to keep starting businesses and generating additional forms of wealth. But many scholars claim that economic inequality is dangerous because it divides society into classes that view one another with suspicion and hostility. The United States tends to allow for more inequality than other industrialized democracies.

Fiscal Policy

A government affects the economy in many ways, including through **fiscal policy,** the way the government taxes its population and spends its resources, and through monetary policy and regulation, which is covered later. All governments require money to operate, so they raise money through taxation. Often governments augment the income generated through taxation by borrowing money. Most governments tax and spend using myriad methods, including spending, borrowing, and running deficits, all of which strongly affect the economy.

THREE STRATEGIES USED BY GOVERNMENTS TO IMPROVE THE ECONOMY		
Fiscal Policy	**Monetary Policy**	**Regulation**
Governments create tax policies and budgets that allow them to allocate resources the most efficiently.	Governments control the amount of money circulating in the economy to control inflation, borrowing, and spending in order to stabilize the economy.	Governments establish economic rules to protect consumers, balance labor and capital, and foster an atmosphere of fair trade.

TAXES

Taxes are seldom neutral. Most tax systems produce winners and losers because governments frequently use their tax policies to encourage—or discourage—certain types of behavior. If a government wants to reward investment, for example, it might cut taxes on capital gains (income earned from selling investments). Alternatively, if a government wishes to discourage drinking alcohol, it might tax liquor at a high rate.

In addition to various taxes on goods and services, most governments rely on one, some, or all of three types of income taxes: progressive, regressive, and flat. Progressive and regressive taxes directly affect income distribution. Regardless of which tax system is used, governments shape people's behavior through the taxes they levy on citizens.

EXAMPLE: The U.S. government has used tax policy to achieve housing goals. For the past fifty years, the federal government has allowed homeowners to deduct mortgage interest from income when determining taxes. This deduction encourages people to buy houses because owning a home can help them save substantially on their tax bill. Because most people who buy houses have a moderate or greater income, the effect of this tax policy is to create a subsidy for housing for the middle and upper classes. In fact, the total cost to the federal government of the home mortgage interest deduction is roughly two and half times what the federal government spends on housing for the poor.

Progressive Taxes

Progressive taxes favor the poor. The rich must pay a higher percentage of their income than the poor in a progressive taxation system. For example, U.S. federal income taxes charge lower income groups about 10 percent of their income, whereas richer people must pay substantially more (more than 20 percent in some cases). People who favor these taxes argue that because the rich can afford to pay more, they should pay more. Progressive taxes attempt to create economic equality. Such policies are sometimes called redistributive because they shift money from one group to another.

Regressive Taxes

Regressive taxes cost the poor a larger portion of their income than they do the rich. Social security taxes are an example of regressive taxes because everyone who earns a paycheck must pay based on their earnings. Wage earners are taxed at a set rate but only on the first $90,000 (approximately). So someone who earns $90,000 pays the same dollar amount as someone who makes $30,000, but the person who earns $30,000 shells out a far bigger percentage of his or her income than the person who earns $90,000. Like progressive taxes, regressive taxes are redistributive, but regressive taxes shift money toward the rich rather than toward the poor.

Flat Taxes

Flat taxes charge everyone the same rate, regardless of income. In practice, there are not many flat taxes in the United States. Even some of the flat tax proposals put forward are not truly flat.

EXAMPLE: Although the United States may not have many flat taxes, other countries do. In fact, during the last ten years, many countries in Eastern Europe (including Russia, Ukraine, Romania, and Georgia) have adopted flat taxes ranging between roughly 10 and 30 percent of income. The governments of these countries instituted the flat tax with the hope that a simpler tax system with fewer loopholes and opportunities for tax shelters would actually increase the amount of taxes they collected from wealthier individuals and corporations.

Other Taxes

Income taxes are certainly not the only kinds of taxes levied by governments. The taxes used by governments include the following:

- **Sales tax** (also known as **excise tax**): A tax paid on purchases; the buyer pays a percentage of the price of the item as tax

- **Luxury tax:** A tax levied on the purchase of extremely expensive luxury items

- **Property tax:** A tax levied on property owners, usually a percentage of the value of the property

User Fees

Governments can also raise money through **user fees,** the money charged to citizens for doing certain things. Examples include fees for using public parks, fees for obtaining licenses (such as a driver's or hunting license), or charging tolls for using certain roads. User fees are a popular way to raise revenue because they are not technically taxes, and they only affect those who use the particular government service.

Tax Credits

Governments use **tax credits** to alleviate the income tax burden for some activities. A tax credit is deducted from the amount of taxes a person owes. A good example is the **Earned Income Tax Credit** program in the United States. The EITC gives lower-income workers back some of the money they paid in payroll taxes. Tax credits are also known as **tax expenditures.**

Loopholes

A **loophole** is a specific provision within a tax law that allows individuals or corporations to reduce the amount they owe in taxes. Politicians put loopholes in tax law in order to reward certain types of behavior (investing in alternate fuel sources, for example). In the United States, the number of loopholes has expanded greatly since the last major tax reform of 1986.

Loopholes and tax credits mean that a person usually does not pay the given tax; he or she usually pays less. The **effective tax rate** is the percentage of income that one actually pays in taxes.

> *EXAMPLE:* In the United States, few people pay the basic rate on their income tax. Every taxpayer is allowed a deduction (standard or itemized), and most are allowed to deduct certain exemptions from their taxable income. Other deductions and credits can reduce the tax burden further. In some extreme cases, people making millions of dollars pay very little in tax because of tax loopholes, deductions, and shelters (a catch-all term for anything that reduces the amount of taxable income).

GOVERNMENT SPENDING AND BORROWING

Government spending and borrowing affect the economy. Most governments spend a great deal of money in their annual budgets. How that money is spent affects people in different ways. Some expenditures create jobs, thereby lessening unemployment. Other expenditures subsidize certain industries, as when a government buys a fleet of cars to aid the automotive industry. Governments also spend money on infrastructure (such as building roads) and defense (such as counterterrorism and the military). Other expenditures, such as worker training, can boost the economy too.

Balanced Budgets and Surpluses

When a government spends the same amount of money it takes in, the government has **balanced the budget.** A surplus arises when a government receives more money than it spends.

The Balanced Budget Amendment

Some fiscal conservatives have attempted to amend the U.S. Constitution to require a balanced federal budget. Many state constitutions mandate a balanced budget, but the federal constitution does not. Attempts to pass a balanced budget amendment have not progressed very far, even though some politicians very much want one.

Deficits and Debt

When a government spends more than it takes in, it runs a **deficit.** Taxes raise only a limited amount of money, so if governments wish to spend more than they have made, they must borrow the difference. The total of all deficits owed by a government is the **national debt** (also called the **public debt**), which must be repaid eventually. Generally, governments tolerate and accept some debt, but too much debt carried for too long causes serious problems.

EXAMPLE: As of July 2006, the United States had a national debt of $8.4 trillion.

Governments most often borrow money by issuing **government bonds.** When a person buys a bond, the government promises to pay back the purchase price plus interest to the owner. In the United States, bonds are sometimes called T Bonds or T Bills because they are issued by the Treasury Department.

A Crisis of Debt

In 1980s, there was an international debt crisis. A number of developing countries had borrowed heavily in the 1970s because of low interest rates. When rates went up in the 1980s, those countries could no longer borrow money and were forced to start paying back what they owed. The huge debts created massive problems—in some cases, a very large chunk of tax revenue went to pay interest on the debt, which led to more borrowing and more debt.

Government Spending and Inflation

Large-scale government spending can increase inflation. If the government buys a lot of goods, it causes an increase in demand for those goods, which causes prices to rise. Sometimes governments are willing to tolerate some rise in inflation to stimulate the economy, but over time, excessive spending and high inflation can create problems.

Government Borrowing and Interest Rates

Government borrowing sometimes creates problems because it drives up interest rates. **Interest,** or the price of borrowing money, goes up when there is an increase in demand for borrowing, which is why heavy government borrowing often drives up interest rates. High interest rates, in turn, hurt the ability of citizens and businesses to borrow money. This chain reaction slows the economy.

$ocial $ecurity

As the baby boomers begin to retire in the United States, social security payments will skyrocket, and the social security fund will be depleted. Most analysts agree that by the time today's college graduates will be getting ready to retire, if not sooner, there will be no money left. In the early twenty-first century, President George W. Bush proposed privatizing social security, so that every person would be responsible for setting aside money to cover his or her retirement rather than having the government do it via paycheck deductions. The proposal lacked the necessary support in Congress, so Bush's social security plan never took off. No solution has yet been reached.

Keynesian Economics

In the early years of the twentieth century, economist John Maynard Keynes argued that governments should step in to actively help the economy. According to **Keynesian economics,** government spending during a recession shortens the length of the recession and keeps the recession from becoming severe. Often this process entailed **deficit spending,** or intentionally spending more money than the government has.

Demand-Side Versus Supply-Side Economics

Keynesian economics is categorized as **demand-side economics.** It stimulates consumer demand by putting more money into consumers' hands in order to improve the economy. In contrast, **supply-side economics** tries to improve the economy by providing big tax cuts to businesses and wealthy individuals (the supply side). These cuts encourage investment, which then creates jobs, so the effect will be felt throughout the economy. Supply-side economics is sometimes called **trickle-down economics.** Although demand-side economics has worked very successfully in much of the world since World War II, some economists and policymakers favor supply-side economics. Also, a number of recent American presidents, most notably Ronald Reagan, have relied on supply-side economics to pull the economy out of recessions.

Monetary Policy

In addition to fiscal policy, a government affects the economy through its **monetary policy,** which controls the amount of money, or currency, in the economy. Money is like any other commodity: When there is more of it, the price of money—that is, interest rates—goes down; when there is less money in the economy, its price goes up. Controlling the amount of money in the economy allows the government to directly influence the economy.

CENTRAL BANKS

Most governments have a **central bank** that controls monetary policy. In the United States, the central bank is called the **Federal Reserve Bank** (also known simply as the Fed). The powers that central banks have vary from state to state.

> *EXAMPLE:* The European Central Bank (ECB) was formed as part of the creation of the European Union. It consists of the main bank plus the central banks of the twenty-five member states of the EU. The bank attempts to control inflation throughout the EU through monetary policy, specifically by monitoring the euro.

The Federal Reserve Bank

The Federal Reserve System was created as part of Franklin Roosevelt's New Deal to reform the American banking system after the Great Depression. The Federal Reserve System consists of twelve branches of the Federal Reserve Bank that are located throughout the country. The system is governed by the Federal Reserve Board, a group of people appointed by the president of the United States and the Senate to determine the national banking policies, including setting interest rates. The Fed is responsible for a number of functions, including:

- Adjusting the supply of money and credit to help the economy

- Ensuring that banks do not overextend themselves

- Facilitating the exchange of cash, checks, and credit

- Setting interest rates

Central Bank Independence

Central banks have varying degrees of independence from the other branches of government. Many scholars think that the central bank should be completely independent from the rest of the government. They reason that the central bank can only make sound economic decisions through independence. Political pressure from the government could hurt the bank's ability to make good policy by demanding short-term fixes that will hurt in the long run. Others argue that the central bank should be under the control of elected officials because the bank, like the rest of the government, needs to respond to the will of the people.

EXAMPLE: The selection of members of the Federal Reserve Board in the United States is one way of trying to resolve the dilemma of how independent the Fed should be. The president nominates and the Senate approves members of the board. However, once someone has been confirmed, he or she serves for a set period and cannot be fired. This job security encourages Federal Reserve Board members to make sound economic policy choices without regard to short-term politics.

CHAPTER 4

The Man, the Myth . . .

An economist named Alan Greenspan served as the chairman of the Federal Reserve Board for almost twenty years, from 1987 to 2006. Greenspan's ability to directly influence the interest rates put him more firmly in control of the American economy than any other individual, which is why political analysts and pundits alike often proclaimed him the most powerful man in the world.

INDIRECT CONTROL

Although monetary policy affects the economy, it does not directly control the economy. Instead, monetary policy encourages certain kinds of behavior. The actions of central banks often lower unemployment and reduce inflation. Lowered interest rates, for example, encourage people to borrow. More borrowing often leads to business investment, which, in turn, creates jobs. But low interest rates do not guarantee that people will borrow. Higher interest rates, in contrast, discourage people from borrowing, which lowers the amount of money being spent and thus reduces inflation. In the long term, monetary policy can be very effective, but in the short term, it may do little. And ultimately, monetary policy cannot force people to borrow money or spend it in ways that help the economy.

Regulatory Policy

In addition to fiscal and monetary policies, a government affects the economy through **regulatory policy,** which aims to limit what can be done in the marketplace. Most governments have some regulations covering a variety of areas, including:

- Banking, insurance, and other financial businesses

- Safety

- Environmental impact

- Minimum wages

> *EXAMPLE:* In the United States, several government agencies
> and independent organizations regulate the market. The
> Federal Reserve Bank, for example, has some power over
> regulatory policy because the Fed tells banks how much
> actual cash must be kept in each bank (this is called
> the reserve rate). The Occupational Health and Safety
> Administration regulates workplace conditions to prevent
> injury. And the Environmental Protection Agency imposes
> limits on toxic emissions.

CHAPTER 4

OVERREGULATION AND DEREGULATION

Sometimes the government does not do a good job of regulating. An excess of regulation leads to **overregulation.** Overregulation can hurt businesses and creates inefficiencies.
Governments usually overregulate out of a desire to increase
equity or promote social justice.

A lack of regulation leads to **deregulation,** or a push to repeal or reduce regulations. Deregulation usually occurs in the
name of boosting economic efficiency. Although it can increase competition, deregulation can sometimes lead to chaos
and hurt consumers.

> *EXAMPLE:* The commercial airline industry in the United
> States was deregulated in the 1970s and 1980s. In general,
> this deregulation resulted in lower prices and more choices
> for consumers. But many airlines now perpetually hover on
> the brink of bankruptcy.

CODETERMINATION

Codetermination is a policy used in some states with strong social democratic parties. Derived in Germany after World War II, codetermination forces large corporations to have substantial representation from the workers on the board of directors. Because workers have direct input into corporate policy, the relationship between workers and management often improves. There have been few labor strikes in Germany as a result.

Sample Test Questions

1. What is political economy? Why do many study it?

2. Describe rational choice.

3. Explain how fighting unemployment can drive up inflation.

4. What are the main complaints of those who object to international financial institutions?

5. What is monetary policy?

    A. Controlling the amount of money in the economy
    B. Raising taxes to fund road-building
    C. A tax that is higher for rich people than for poor people
    D. The ability to print money

6. How can fiscal policy affect interest rates?

    A. Government borrowing can drive them up.
    B. Taxes drive them up.
    C. Taxes drive them down.
    D. Expenditures drive them down.

7. What is Keynesian economics?

A. The belief in laissez-faire economic policy
B. The use of central planning to promote growth
C. The claim that global trade is damaging to workers
D. The belief that the government should "prime the pump" to get the economy going

8. What is a redistributive policy?

A. A policy that benefits the rich
B. Any monetary policy
C. A policy that takes money from some people and gives it to others
D. A policy that is popular

9. Which best describes a command economy?

A. It uses the free market to determine prices.
B. It uses central planning to determine the economy.
C. It is usually associated with monarchies.
D. It produces tremendous economic growth.

10. Which of the following is not a method states use to affect their economies?

A. Monetary policy
B. Command policy
C. Fiscal policy
D. Regulatory policy

CHAPTER 4

ANSWERS

1. Political economy is the study of the interaction of politics and economics. It is widely studied because of the importance of economic growth and distribution.

2. Rational choice is a method of analyzing and understanding human behavior by assuming that people act in an economically rational way (i.e., they work to maximize their gain).

3. Two of the best ways for the government to fight unemployment are to spend more money and to lower interest rates. But both of these methods increase demand, which drives up prices, and therefore inflation.

4. There are a number of different objections to international financial institutions. Some believe that global trade hurts the environment; others fear that it will cause a loss of jobs; others see the whole system as biased in favor of developed states.

5. A

6. A

7. D

8. C

9. B

10. B

Suggested Reading

• Frieden, Jeffry. *Debt, Development, and Democracy*. Princeton, NJ: Princeton University Press, 1991.

This book examines the role of debt on developing states.

• Kennedy Paul. *The Rise and Fall of Great Powers*. New York: Vintage, 1989.

A more recent take on the ideas raised by Mancur Olson in *The Rise and Decline of Nations*.

• Keynes, John Maynard. *The General Theory of Employment, Interest, and Money.* 1936. Reprint, Amherst, New York: Prometheus Books, 1997.

One of the founding documents of Keynesian economics, written by the man himself.

• Landes, David. *The Wealth and Poverty of Nations: Why Some Are So Rich and Some So Poor.* New York: Norton, 1999.

This book theorizes about why some nations succeed economically while others fail repeatedly.

• Marx, Karl. *Das Kapital.* Translated by Ben Fowkes. 1867. Reprint, New York: Penguin, 1992.

A dense and difficult account of capitalist economics from the father of modern socialism.

• Olson, Mancur. *The Rise and Decline of Nations.* New Haven, Conn.: Yale University Press, 1982.

A classic political economy work in which Olson explores how a strong economy positively and negatively affects a society.

• Smith, Adam. *The Wealth of Nations.* 1776. Reprint, Indianapolis: Hackett, 1993.

Another classic work, which deals with free-market economies and capitalism.

Useful Websites

• www.epa.gov

The website of the Environmental Protection Agency, a key regulatory agency.

CHAPTER 4

- www.federalreserve.gov

The website of the Federal Reserve Board.

- www.imf.org

The website of the International Monetary Fund.

- www.publicdebt.treas.gov

The United States Department of the Treasury keeps a running tally of the U.S. national debt, updated daily, on this website.

- www.whitehouse.gov/OMB

The website of the Office of Management and Budget, which helps the president put the budget proposal together. The site includes the most recent federal budgets.

- www.worldbank.org

The website of the World Bank.

POLITICAL CULTURE AND PUBLIC OPINION

5

Overview

Different nations have different languages, faiths, ethnicities, traditions, histories, and worldviews. As a result, the government created by each nation is distinct and unique. Countries may create similar governments—there are many democracies in the world, for example—but no two political systems are exactly identical. Moreover, the ways people interact with their government differ from country to country as well, so no two political cultures are truly similar, nor is public opinion the same from country to country.

What Is Political Culture?

A **political culture** is a set of attitudes and practices held by a people that shapes their political behavior. It includes moral judgments, political myths, beliefs, and ideas about what makes for a good society. A political culture is a reflection of a government, but it also incorporates elements of history and tradition that may predate the current regime. Political cultures matter because they shape a population's political perceptions and actions. Governments can help shape political culture and public opinion through education, public events, and commemoration of the past. Political cultures vary greatly from state to state and sometimes even within a state. Generally speaking, however, political culture remains more or less the same over time.

EXAMPLE: The United States and Great Britain are both democracies, but each has a distinct political culture. The American government derives its powers from a written constitution drafted by men who feared monarchs and strong central governments, which is why they divided the federal government into three distinct branches. Also, the American political system is dominated by two political parties. Great Britain, in contrast, has a long history of monarchy and has never had a written constitution. Even though the current monarch holds the official title of head of state, her powers are nominal, leaving Parliament— the legislative body—as the dominant element of the government. And unlike the United States, Great Britain currently has nearly half a dozen political parties that regularly seat candidates in Parliament.

Regional Culture

Even within the United States, political culture varies from place to place. For much of the twentieth century, southern politicians were reputed to be slow-acting and polite, whereas northern politicians were seen as efficient but abrupt and sometimes rude. This belief led President John F. Kennedy to once lament that Washington, D.C., had the charm of a northern city and the efficiency of a southern one.

CITIZENSHIP

Political culture is connected to notions of **citizenship** because political culture frequently includes an idea of what makes people good citizens. A **citizen** is a legal member of a political community, with certain rights and obligations. Because each country has its own requirements for citizenship and attendant rights, the definition of "citizen" varies around the world.

EXAMPLE: Not surprisingly, different countries have different criteria for citizenship. France automatically bestows citizenship on anyone born in French territory via *jus soli* (Latin for "right by territory"). Germany grants citizenship via *jus sanguines* (Latin for "right by blood") to people who have a German parent. Israel's Law of Return, meanwhile, allows any Jew to move permanently to Israel and become a citizen. The United States grants citizenship rights both to people who are born in American territory and to people who have an American parent.

Aristotle and Citizenship

The Greek philosopher Aristotle was probably the first person to puzzle over what makes someone a citizen in his treatise *Politics* (c. 335–323 BCE). He reasoned that living in a particular place does not automatically make a person a citizen because, in his day (as in ours) resident aliens and immigrants often lived in a country without becoming citizens. In the end, Aristotle defined a citizen as one who shares in the offices and power of a regime (even if only in a small way). So, a tyranny has one citizen, whereas a democracy has many citizens.

Characteristics of Good Citizens

A good citizen lives up to the ideals of the regime and embodies much of what a particular political culture considers important. An American who lives an exemplary life but who does not work to help the community will probably be viewed as a good person but not as a good citizen. Instead, Americans expect good citizens to help others and to make the community a better place through active participation in public life. In the United States, a good citizen is often expected to do some or all of the following:

- Vote in elections

- Obey all local, state, and federal laws

- Pay taxes

- Be informed about political issues

- Volunteer to help less fortunate people

- Demonstrate patriotism by respecting the flag, singing the national anthem, and knowing the Pledge of Allegiance

- Recycle

- Help the community when needed

Stereotypes

Political scientists seem to be in a quandary. On the one hand, they make generalizations about politics and people in order to gain a broader understanding. On the other hand, political scientists do not want to rely on, or perpetuate, stereotypes. Finding a balance between these two is difficult. Scholars must carefully examine their use of language and data in an attempt to avoid stereotyping.

POLITICAL CULTURE AND CHANGE

Political culture changes over time, but these changes often happen slowly. People frequently become set in their ways and refuse to alter their attitudes on significant issues. Sometimes it can take generations for major shifts to occur in a nation's political culture.

EXAMPLE: One example of the ways in which American political culture has been slow to change concerns the rights of minorities. The Voting Rights Act of 1965 authorized federal troops to supervise balloting in federal elections in the South in order to protect the voting rights of black Americans. Even though the bill passed forty years ago, many government officials fear that racial tensions in the South could still threaten the political freedoms of blacks, which is why Congress and President George W. Bush reauthorized the Voting Rights Act in 2006.

Nation-Building and Political Culture

Political culture has presented great difficulties to the military forces in Iraq and Afghanistan engaged in nation-building during the early years of the twenty-first century. The United States is trying to build liberal democracies in these states, but in both places, long-held attitudes toward women and other ethnic groups, along with habits of obedience shaped by years of tyranny, have interfered. As a result, establishing democracies in these states could take a very long time.

Political Socialization

People acquire political culture through a process known as **political socialization.** Although the bulk of political socialization occurs during childhood, adults continue to be socialized. Political socialization occurs in many ways:

- **Family:** Young children usually spend far more time with their families than with anyone else and thus tend to acquire the family's habits, beliefs, behaviors, and attitudes. For this reason, family tends to be the most important source of political socialization. Families mostly impart political culture unintentionally by acting as examples for the children. Very often, people end up with political beliefs similar to those of their parents.

- **School:** Most children learn about their country at school, usually through a curriculum known as **civic education.** This curriculum trains young people to be good citizens, often via history, government, and social studies. Although these lessons are usually basic, many of the key ideas and values of a society are imparted through school.

    EXAMPLE: Most students learn about U.S. history at a young age, but textbooks and teachers tend to simplify the history and present it in a positive light. For example, the end of racial segregation is usually discussed as a sign of the progress America has made toward equality and liberty.

- **Peers:** At all ages, friends and acquaintances will influence one's beliefs.

- **Religion:** Different religious traditions have very different values, and one's faith often significantly influences one's political views.

    EXAMPLE: Roman Catholicism has a well-defined set of positions on many political issues, ranging from abortion to capital punishment to social justice. Although not all Catholics oppose abortion or favor more welfare programs, many do as a result of their religious beliefs.

- **Social and economic class:** The social class to which one belongs shapes one's views.

CHAPTER 5

EXAMPLE: Blue-collar workers in the United States tend to favor liberal economic policies but usually oppose many liberal social policies. For much of the twentieth century, economic issues seemed more important to many blue-collar workers, so they tended to vote for the Democrats. In the last few decades, though, social issues have taken on new importance, and an increasing number of blue-collar workers have voted Republican.

- **Minority status:** Members of a minority group sometimes feel like outsiders, and this feeling of isolation and alienation affects their attitudes toward society and government. This is particularly true when the minority group is treated either better or worse than others in society.

- **Media:** The power of media is increasing with the spread of 24-hour cable news networks, talk radio, the Internet, and the seeming omnipresence of personal audio and video devices, so the influence of the media on political socialization is no longer confined to the young.

- **Key events:** A major political event can shape an entire generation's attitudes toward its nation and government.

EXAMPLE: World War II defined the attitudes of many Americans, especially those who served in it. Many veterans became dedicated to living up to the ideals professed in the war. Twenty years later, the Vietnam War would have a similarly important impact, fostering skepticism of foreign military operations. In the 1970s, the Watergate scandal instilled a profound mistrust of government in many people.

THE ROLE OF GOVERNMENT

The government plays a role in political socialization in a variety of ways. It determines the policies and curricula, including what books students may read, for public schools. The government also regulates the media, which affects what we see and hear. In the United States, broadcast television programs cannot contain nudity or profane language, and the government also mandates a certain amount of "family-friendly" programming per week. These choices have a subtle effect on viewers: We learn that bad language is inappropriate and that family is an essential part of American life and therefore American political culture. Similarly, governments frequently stage parades and celebrations to commemorate important events and people in history.

> *EXAMPLE:* Every American state requires students to pass tests in order to graduate from high school. In some states, the tests include citizenship exams, which assess students' knowledge of government and political culture. To pass the tests, students take courses in these topics, which allows the states to emphasize what they consider important by regulating the curricula. The states sometimes differ greatly in what they teach.

In authoritarian and totalitarian regimes, the government often takes active measures to inculcate loyalty, especially in younger people. The Nazis, for example, created the Hitler Youth, which instilled allegiance to Adolf Hitler in young people in Germany during the Third Reich. Similar programs existed in the former Soviet Union.

Plato and Socialization

In *The Republic* (390 BCE), Plato writes about the creation of a good aristocratic regime. But most of the book describes the educational system and discusses what will be taught to the young. This emphasis shows Plato's understanding of the importance of socialization: He argued that raising a generation indoctrinated with the values of the regime was essential to the regime's survival. In fact, Plato even claims that, in order for the good republic to succeed, the city founders must expel everyone over the age of ten because their attitudes have already been shaped and cannot be changed.

Social Capital

Social capital is the mutual trust and cooperation that arises from the web of connections among people involved in organizations and community groups. For the most part, private activities, not government ones, foster social capital. The term **civil society** is sometimes used as a synonym for the relationships that create social capital. In a civil society, social capital flows easily between people.

CREATING SOCIAL CAPITAL

Activities that can build social capital include the following:

- Participating in the local parent-teacher association

- Joining a civic organization, such as the Elks or the Kiwanis Club

- Volunteering in the neighborhood or around the community

- Forming a neighborhood watch

- Donating old clothes or goods

- Contributing to a food bank

- Joining a church or synagogue group

- Belonging to a bridge team, craft club, or other type of common-interest group

Bowling Alone

Robert Putnam's successful book *Bowling Alone: The Collapse and Revival of American Community* (2001) put the issue of social capital into the context of popular culture. Putnam noticed that bowling leagues had declined significantly in the last few decades of the twentieth century. People still bowled, but as individuals and informal groups, not as part of a league. This change prompted Putnam to worry that the decline of membership in community groups was eroding America's social capital. The book prompted a great deal of debate and some controversy over Putnam's conclusions that America's social capital was rapidly declining.

SOCIAL CAPITAL AND DEMOCRACY

In a democratic society, people must be willing to trust others and tolerate those with whom they disagree. Without these attitudes, democracy can fail, because democracy is ultimately a cooperative form of government. Many political scientists regard social capital as essential to democracy because social capital forges bonds between members of the community. These bonds enable people to readily join together. Also, working with others helps build a sense of community and trust among citizens, which, in turn, creates more social capital.

Social Capital and Democratization

One of the most difficult tasks for any democratizing country is the building of civil society. Authoritarian regimes discourage civil society because civil society can form the basis of resistance to the government. These governments instill fear and mistrust within their citizens, often turning groups and individuals against one another. New democracies sometimes have trouble building community trust and tolerance because their citizens are not used to working together in civil society. For this reason, nations that seek to help other nations democratize must focus much energy on creating social capital and building civil societies.

Political Participation

Political participation is any activity that shapes, affects, or involves the political sphere. Political participation ranges from voting to attending a rally to committing an act of terrorism to sending a letter to a representative. Broadly speaking, there are three types of participation:

1. **Conventional participation:** Activities that we expect of good citizens. For most people, participation occurs every few years at election time. People strongly committed to politics are more likely to participate on a regular basis.

   EXAMPLE: Conventional political participation includes voting, volunteering for a political campaign, making a campaign donation, belonging to activist groups, and serving in public office.

2. **Unconventional participation:** Activities that are legal but often considered inappropriate. Young people, students, and those with grave concerns about a regime's policies are most likely to engage in unconventional participation.

   EXAMPLE: Unconventional political participation includes signing petitions, supporting boycotts, and staging demonstrations and protests.

3. **Illegal participation:** activities that break the law. Most of the time, people resort to illegal participation only when legal means have failed to create significant political change.

   EXAMPLE: Illegal political participation includes political assassination, terrorism, and sabotaging an opponent's campaign through theft or vandalism.

The Watergate Scandal

The Watergate scandal, which brought down the presidency of Richard M. Nixon in 1974, involved illegal political participation. The Nixon campaign, working actively with the Nixon Administration, used espionage and subversion against its opponents. For example, Nixon supporters forged letters from opposing candidates, such as the infamous "Canuck Letter," to discredit those candidates. The scandal got its name from the Watergate offices of the Democratic National Committee, which members of the Nixon campaign had broken into in order to plant spying devices and to steal files.

WHY PEOPLE PARTICIPATE

Most democratic citizens feel that some level of political participation, particularly conventional participation, is admirable and acceptable. But political participation can be hard: One must find time, and perhaps money, in order to participate. So why do people do it? People participate in politics out of a sense of the following:

- **Idealism:** Some participate because they believe strongly in a particular idea.

- **Responsibility:** For many, participation is a responsibility of democratic citizenship.

- **Self-interest:** A person might work to promote issues and causes that personally profit that person.

- **Enjoyment:** Some simply enjoy public activity, either because of the activity itself or because of the friends they make while politically engaged.

CHAPTER 5

THE PARADOX OF PARTICIPATION

Rational choice theorists have argued that participation, particularly voting, is irrational. In a large country, the probability that one's vote will decide the outcome of an election is microscopic. Because participation has costs (time to vote, effort to learn about the candidates and issues, and so on), the costs of voting outweigh the benefits. In other words, voting does not make sense for people as an activity. Another way to think about this issue is to consider the person who votes because he or she desires to have an impact on the government. If he or she votes out of a sense that the one vote will make a difference, then this person will be sorely disappointed. The truth is that one vote does not make a difference. At the same time, however, if everyone who votes ceased to believe in the power of voting to effect change, then no one would turn out for elections and the democratic process would stop functioning. Political scientists call this phenomenon the **paradox of participation.**

NONPARTICIPATION

In some countries, large parts of the population do not participate in politics at all. In the United States, for example, only about half of all eligible people vote in presidential elections. Such nonparticipation signifies a number of attitudes:

- **Contentment:** Lack of participation indicates satisfaction with the status quo—if they were upset about an issue, people would participate.

- **Freedom:** In a democratic society, people have the freedom to not participate.

- **Apathy:** Many people do not know much about politics and do not care.

- **Alienation:** People do not participate because they feel that no one in power listens to their views and that the government is, at best, indifferent to them.

Public Opinion

Public opinion consists of the views held by the population of a state that influence those in power. In a democratic state, politicians must listen to public opinion if they wish to keep their jobs. Dissatisfied constituents can vote out those who ignore their views. But regimes with other types of governments also need to pay attention to public opinion. If the public overwhelmingly opposes the government, the regime could be in serious danger of revolution or collapse.

ASSESSING PUBLIC OPINION

We learn about public opinion through **polling,** which asks people their views and then compiles the results. Politicians and pundits in many countries rely on public opinion polls, and the media frequently reports on polls. **Sampling** a subset of the population allows **pollsters,** or the people who create and take the polls, to get a sense of overarching concerns and interests within a large population. Rather than polling every citizen, an expensive and time-consuming process, polls use **samples.** Pollsters hope that the opinions of the sample accurately reflect the population as a whole. Just as one does not need to taste every bite of stew to know that it needs more salt, one need not poll every person to learn public opinion.

Good and Bad Samples

To make sure that their poll results are accurate, pollsters seek good samples. The most obvious way to get a good sample is to include lots of people. But including more people does not guarantee that the poll will be accurate. Instead, a sample must be **representative**—that is, the sample must have the same basic characteristics as the population. If the population has a 15 percent poverty rate, for example, the sample should have a roughly equal portion of poor people. Pollsters have a number of techniques to ensure a representative sample, and they rely on statistical methods to measure the probability that a poll is accurate.

CHAPTER 5

Pollsters rely heavily on probability and randomness to increase the chance of getting a good sample. In a **probability sample,** each person in the population has a known chance of being chosen as part of the sample. When pollsters assign each person an equal chance of being selected, they are using **random selection.**

Sampling error results from bad samples. A poll that falls prey to sampling error will inaccurately measure public opinion. A common source of sampling error is a **skewed sample,** one that does not match the population. Some popular types of polling—asking people as they walk down the street, for example, or online polls—produce very skewed samples and are therefore unreliable.

The *Literary Digest* Poll

One of the most notorious examples of a bad sample is the 1936 presidential election poll conducted by the *Literary Digest,* a notable magazine of the era. The sample numbered more than a million people, but it ended up very wrong: The poll predicted that Alfred Landon would defeat Franklin Roosevelt, but Roosevelt won easily. The poll was wrong because its sample was skewed. Pollsters contacted people in phone books, as well as people with registered automobiles. But during the Great Depression, rich people were the only ones with phones and cars. Thus, the poll contained responses from far too many rich people and not nearly enough from other social classes.

INFLUENCES ON PUBLIC OPINION

Many factors affect public opinion:

- **Politicians:** Many officials actively campaign to generate support among the public. They give speeches and interviews, stage rallies, and listen to constituents.

- **Media:** The news media covers all major political events extensively. Indeed, sometimes it seems that the media creates important political events by choosing to cover them so much. Because the vast majority of people get their political information from the media, it has a huge impact.

- **Socioeconomic status:** Most political and economic events affect people unevenly, so one's social and economic status naturally affects one's views. Wealthy people are more likely than poor people to support a budget that cuts taxes on capital gains, for example, because they would benefit more from the tax cut.

- **Major events:** Any significant event—a war, an economic downturn, or a diplomatic success, for example—can influence people's views.

  > *EXAMPLE:* In the United States, whenever a foreign crisis arises, support for the president shoots up dramatically. Political scientists call this increase in popularity the **rally 'round the flag** effect. The effect might not always last a long time, but in the short run, the president's popularity goes up.

- **Opinion leaders:** Political scientists call a person whose views on an issue can affect the views of others an **opinion leader.** Often, opinion leaders are prominent members of the community and pay more attention to politics than most people.

  > *EXAMPLE:* The Internet has created a new type of opinion leader called a *blogger* (short for web logger). Many people read the same political blogs every day and are strongly influenced by what they read. Politicians have begun to court bloggers, going so far as to invite them to conventions and to grant them interviews in an attempt to win the opinion leaders over to their side.

CHAPTER 5

Media Saturation

In the last twenty years, the media has become a bigger part of our lives. Twenty-four-hour news networks allow people to tune in any time. At the same time, the networks must find something to fill all those hours—and to outdo one another—so the networks often seek sensational stories. Talk radio has also become extremely popular. Many people rely on talk radio for much of their news, even though many talk radio hosts are openly partisan. Escaping the media often seems impossible: There always seems to be a television, radio, or Internet stream playing in the background of our daily lives.

Elitism Versus Pluralism

How much does public opinion really matter? There are two views regarding the importance of public opinion:

- **Elitism:** Society is run by a few people at the top, including important politicians and businesspeople, so public opinion matters very little. What the masses think does not matter, and leaders can shape public opinion to suit their purposes.

- **Pluralism:** There are many different centers of power, so public opinion matters a great deal. Leaders may have more power than the masses, but they must heed mass opinion if they wish to remain in office.

Sample Test Questions

1. What is political culture? Why is it important?

2. Define *political socialization*.

3. What factors shape public opinion?

4. True or false: When polling, the only thing to worry about is getting a large sample.

5. True or false: Social capital is created when people join community groups and volunteer organizations.

6. What would staging a protest be considered in the United States?

A. Illegal participation
B. Unconventional participation
C. Conventional participation
D. Socialization

7. What does the paradox of participation state?

A. It is not rational to participate, yet people do.
B. People who don't participate are lazy.
C. Participation is a noble thing.
D. The costs of participation are too high.

8. What is a citizen?

A. Someone who lives in a country
B. Someone who is a legal member of a political community
C. Someone who votes
D. Someone who supports the government

9. Which of the following is *not* a factor of political socialization?

A. Education
B. Polling
C. Family
D. Media

10. Which of the following best describes a representative sample?

A. It is very large.
B. It guarantees an accurate poll.
C. It affects participation.
D. It resembles the population as a whole.

ANSWERS

1. A political culture is the set of beliefs, values, shared myths, and notions of a polity held by a group of people. It is important because it affects how those people will behave in the political realm.

2. Political socialization is the process by which people acquire the habits and beliefs of a political culture.

3. Many factors influence public opinion, including the media, efforts by politicians, major events, and one's socioeconomic status.

4. False

5. True

6. B

7. A

8. B

9. B

10. D

Suggested Reading

- Almond, Gabriel, and Sidney Verba. *The Civic Culture: Political Attitudes and Democracy in Five Nations.* Princeton, NJ: Princeton University Press, 1963.

A comparison of the political cultures in England, Germany, Italy, Mexico, and the United States.

- Erikson, Robert, Norman Luttbeg, and Kent Tedin. *American Public Opinion.* 5th ed. Englewood Cliffs, NJ: Prentice Hall, 1994.

An outstanding review of scholarly literature on public opinion.

- Jaros, Dean. *Socialization to Politics.* New York: Praeger, 1973.

A brief account of political socialization.

- Lippmann, Walter. *Public Opinion.* New York: Simon & Schuster, 1997.

Lippmann, a renowned journalist, studies the way public opinion does—and does not—affect the government.

- Niemi, Richard G., and Jane Junn. *Civic Education: What Makes Students Learn.* New Haven, Conn.: Yale University Press, 1998.

A scholarly look at civic education.

- Orwell, George. *1984.* New York: Harcourt Brace Jovanovich, 1949.

A famous novel of a future dystopia, Orwell portrays political socialization taken to the extreme by a totalitarian government.

- Putnam, Robert. *Bowling Alone: The Collapse and Revival of American Community.* New York: Simon & Schuster, 2001.

CHAPTER 5

Putnam's book (based on an earlier article) brought the debate over social capital to national attention.

- de Tocqueville, Alexis. *Democracy in America.* New York: Schocken, 1961.

One of the most famous accounts of American political culture, it is still relevant today.

- Wills, Garry. *A Necessary Evil: A History of American Distrust of Government.* 1999. Reprint, New York: Simon & Schuster, 2002.

One of America's most prominent public intellectuals discusses American wariness toward government.

- Wilson, James Q. *The Moral Sense.* New York: Free Press, 1995.

A prominent political scientist uses a cross-disciplinary approach to study how people acquire moral beliefs and habits.

Useful Websites

- www.bettertogether.org

A page that gives suggestions to help build social capital and combat social apathy in the United States. The project grew out of a 1996 seminar given at Harvard University by Robert Putnam.

- www.gallup.com

This website belongs to the best-known polling company in the United States.

- www.icpsr.umich.edu/GSS
  www.umich.edu/~nes/nesguide/nesguide.htm

Two websites run by the Inter-University Consortium for Political and Social Research, one of the most respected public opinion polling groups in the United States. The first, the General Social Survey, covers a broad range of matters, including demographics, economic behavior, and general views of social events. The second, the National Election Survey, is an in-depth study of voting behavior conducted every two years.

- www.people-press.org

The Pew Center for the People and the Press does extensive polling on a wide variety of issues. They post not only the results but also their raw data online.

- www.politicsol.com/quiz.html

A quiz to see how much you know about American politics. How well socialized are you?

- www2.excelgov.org

The website for the Partnership for Trust in Government, which tries to build up social capital and public trust by sponsoring educational programs and handing out literature about the American government.

CHAPTER 5

.

INTERNATIONAL POLITICS

6

Overview

Governments not only interact with the people they rule but also with other governments—to trade, to share ideas, to work together to solve global problems, and to resolve disputes. Political scientists have been analyzing international relations—relations between states—for centuries, but never more so than during the twentieth century, as scholars tried to explain the reasons for and explore the aftermath of World Wars I and II and the Cold War that followed.

Although numerous international agreements and institutions exist to facilitate smooth relations among the nearly 200 countries in the world, international politics can still be extremely violent. Even though people have fought one another for millennia, political scientists still do not know exactly what causes people and states to go to war, start revolutions, or commit acts of terrorism. Identifying both immediate and long-term causes and consequences of political violence, as well as thinking about the impact of this violence on the international system, has become an important part of political science.

History of the International System

States engage with one another in an environment known as the **international system.** All states are considered to be sovereign, and some states are more powerful than others. The system has a number of informal rules about how things should be done, but these rules are not binding. International relations have existed as long as states themselves. But the modern international system under which we live today is only a few centuries old. Significant events have marked the milestones in the development of the international system.

THE PEACE OF WESTPHALIA (1648)

In 1648, the Peace of Westphalia, which ended the Thirty Years' War between Catholic states and Protestant states in western and central Europe, established our modern international system. It declared that the sovereign leader of each nation-state could do as she or he wished within its borders and established the state as the main actor in global politics. From that point forward, the international system has consisted primarily of relations among nation-states.

SHIFTING BALANCES OF POWER (1600–1800)

In the seventeenth and eighteenth centuries, the nation-state emerged as the dominant political unit of the international system. A series of powerful states dominated Europe, with the great powers rising and falling. Weaker states often banded together to prevent the dominant power from becoming too strong, a practice known as preserving the **balance of power.** Frequent wars and economic competition marked this era. Some nations—notably France and England—were powerful through most of the modern age, but some—such as Spain and the Ottoman Empire—shrank in power over time.

EMERGENCE OF NATIONALISM (1800–1945)

The nineteenth century brought two major changes to the international system:

1. Nationalism emerged as a strong force, allowing nation-states to grow even more powerful.

2. Italy and Germany became unified countries, which altered the balance of military and economic power in Europe.

The problems raised by the unification of Germany contributed to World War I (1914–1918). In the aftermath of the war, the international system changed dramatically again. The major powers of Europe had suffered greatly, whereas the United States began to come out of its isolation and transform into a global power. At the same time, the end of the Ottoman and Austro-Hungarian empires created a series of new nations, and the rise of communism in Russia presented problems for other nations. These factors contributed to the Treaty of Versailles, the rise of Nazism and communism, and World War II (1939–1945).

CHAPTER 6

NEW WORLD ORDERS (1945–PRESENT)

The end of World War II marked a decisive shift in the global system. After the war, only two great world powers remained: the United States and the Soviet Union. Although some other important states existed, almost all states were understood within the context of their relations with the two superpowers. This global system was called **bipolar** because the system centered on two great powers.

Since the end of the Cold War and the fall of the Soviet Union, the nature of the world has changed again. Only one superpower remains, leading some scholars to label the new international system **unipolar.** Others point to the increasing economic power of some European and Asian states and label the new system **multipolar.** To some extent, both terms are accurate. The United States has the world's most powerful military, which supports the unipolar view, but the U.S. economy is not as powerful, relative to the rest of the world, lending credence to the multipolar view.

CONTEMPORARY INTERNATIONAL SYSTEMS			
System	**Number of Nations with Power**	**Nations with Power**	**Dates**
Unipolar	One	United States	Post-1989
Bipolar	Two	United States and the Soviet Union	1945–1989
Multi-polar	Several	United States, United Kingdom, France, Russia, Germany, Italy, Japan	Pre–World War I
		United States, European Union, China, India	Post-1989

A Plethora of Politics

Political scientists usually use the terms *international politics* and *global politics* synonymously, but technically the terms have different meanings. **International politics,** strictly speaking, refers to relationships between states. **Global politics,** in contrast, refers to relationships among states and other interest groups, such as global institutions, corporations, and political activists. **Comparative politics** seeks to understand how states work by comparing them to one another. While international relations studies how states *relate* to one another, comparative politics *compare* the internal workings of a state, its political institutions, its political culture, and the political behavior of its citizens.

Theories of International Relations

A **theory of international relations** is a set of ideas that explains how the international system works. Unlike an ideology, a theory of international relations is (at least in principle) backed up with concrete evidence. The two major theories of international relations are realism and liberalism.

National Interest

Most theories of international relations are based on the idea that states always act in accordance with their **national interest,** or the interests of that particular state. State interests often include self-preservation, military security, economic prosperity, and influence over other states. Sometimes two or more states have the same national interest. For example, two states might both want to foster peace and economic trade. And states with diametrically opposing national interests might try to resolve their differences through negotiation or even war.

CHAPTER 6

REALISM

According to **realism,** states work only to increase their own power relative to that of other states. Realism also claims the following:

- The world is a harsh and dangerous place. The only certainty in the world is power. A powerful state will always be able to outdo—and outlast—weaker competitors. The most important and reliable form of power is military power.

- A state's primary interest is self-preservation. Therefore, the state must seek power and must always protect itself

- There is no overarching power that can enforce global rules or punish bad behavior.

- Moral behavior is very risky because it can undermine a state's ability to protect itself.

- The international system itself drives states to use military force and to war. Leaders may be moral, but they must not let moral concerns guide foreign policy.

- International organizations and law have no power or force; they exist only as long as states accept them.

Politicians have practiced realism as long as states have existed. Most scholars and politicians during the Cold War viewed international relations through a realist lens. Neither the United States nor the Soviet Union trusted the other, and each sought allies to protect itself and increase its political and military influence abroad. Realism has also featured prominently in the administration of George W. Bush.

Machiavelli

One of the best-known realist thinkers is the notorious Niccolo Machiavelli. In his book *The Prince* (1513), he advised rulers to use deceit and violence as tools against other states. Moral goals are so dangerous, he wrote, that to act morally will bring about disaster. He also gave advice about how to deal with conflicts among neighboring states and how to defend one's homeland. Machiavelli's name has become synonymous with nasty and brutal politics.

LIBERALISM

Liberalism emphasizes that the broad ties among states have both made it difficult to define national interest and decreased the usefulness of military power. Liberalism developed in the 1970s as some scholars began arguing that realism was outdated. Increasing globalization, the rapid rise in communications technology, and the increase in international trade meant that states could no longer rely on simple power politics to decide matters. Liberal approaches to international relations are also called *theories of complex interdependence*. Liberalism claims the following:

- The world is a harsh and dangerous place, but the consequences of using military power often outweigh the benefits. International cooperation is therefore in the interest of every state.

- Military power is not the only form of power. Economic and social power matter a great deal too. Exercising economic power has proven more effective than exercising military power.

- Different states often have different primary interests.

- International rules and organizations can help foster cooperation, trust, and prosperity.

CHAPTER 6

EXAMPLE: Relations among the major Western powers fit a model of complex interdependence very well. The United States has significant disagreements with its European and Asian allies over trade and policy, but it is hard to imagine a circumstance in which the United States would use military power against any of these allies. Instead, the United States relies on economic pressure and incentives to achieve its policy aims.

Idealism

Idealism is a specific school of liberalism that stresses the need for states to pursue moral goals and to act ethically in the international arena. Idealists believe that behavior considered immoral on an interpersonal level is also immoral in foreign policy. Therefore, idealists argue that dishonesty, trickery, and violence should be shunned. In the United States, idealism has usually been associated with the Democratic Party since World War I.

EXAMPLE: As he negotiated the treaty to end World War I in 1918, Woodrow Wilson worked to promote democracy and national self-determination. Wilson's idealism led him to push hard for the creation of the League of Nations, an international organization that would fight aggression and protect the weak from the strong, in 1919. Scholars use the term *Wilsonian* to describe a person or group who advocates promoting democracy overseas in the name of idealism.

International Agreements and Law

In order to make the global system less chaotic and unpredictable, states often make agreements with one another to modify their behavior. **International agreements** are treaties signed by a number of states that establish global rules of conduct. Some agreements focus on single issues, whereas others cover many areas. Theoretically, international agreements benefit the states that sign them. States that break these rules—sometimes called **rogue states**—are usually treated with wariness by the rest of the world.

EXAMPLE: The United States has identified North Korea, Iran, Syria, and Cuba as rogue states because they have continually threatened international security by harboring terrorists and fostering the development of weapons of mass destruction. Afghanistan and Iraq were considered rogue states before the American invasions in the early twenty-first century. As soon as a state begins cooperating and participating in the international community, it loses its status as a rogue state. In 2002, the U.S. Department of State removed Libya from its list of rogue states after the Libyan government voluntarily agreed to renounce terrorism and violence.

International law is the collection of rules and regulations that have evolved over the past few centuries. These rules define the rights and obligations of states. Sometimes treaties codify and formalize international law, but just as often, international law arises from custom and habit. The International Court of Justice, in the Netherlands, is the judicial body of the United Nations and is responsible for resolving disputes among states.

EXAMPLE: In 2006, the International Court of Justice heard testimony relating to a boundary dispute between Nicaragua and Colombia. Another case on its docket concerned charges of genocide brought by Bosnia against Serbia; in early 2007, the court ruled in favor of Bosnia, deciding that Serbia had failed to prevent genocide in Bosnia.

CHAPTER 6

THE EFFECTIVENESS OF INTERNATIONAL LAW

A key dispute among political scientists concerns the effectiveness of international law. Realists argue that because there is no international police force to enforce international law, the law has no real power. States only obey international law when it is in their interest to do so. Liberalists, however, dispute this idea, contending that there are real consequences to breaking international law—such as sanctions and even military occupation—and that international organizations have a measurable impact on global relations.

INTERNATIONAL TREATIES

International treaties serve as an important part of international law. States sign treaties to end wars, protect their interests, and make international law. The treaties listed in the chart below have significantly contributed to the structure of the international systems.

SIGNIFICANT INTERNATIONAL TREATIES		
Treaty	Date Signed	Purpose/Effect
Sykes-Picot Agreement	1916	Set boundaries that still exist today for nations in the Middle East
Treaty of Versailles	1919	Ended World War I; its punitive treatment of Germany set the stage for World War II
Munich Agreement	1938	Gave the Sudetenland (part of Czechoslovakia) to Germany in exchange for a promise of no more expansion; its violation led to World War II
United Nations Charter	1945	Created the United Nations

SIGNIFICANT INTERNATIONAL TREATIES (CONT'D)		
Treaty	**Date Signed**	**Purpose/Effect**
General Agreement on Tariffs and Trade	1947	Greatly reduced tariffs and boosted trade
North Atlantic Treaty	1949	Created the North Atlantic Treaty Organization (NATO), an alliance of Western powers dedicated to preventing communist expansion
Convention on the Prevention and Punishment of the Crime of Genocide	1951	Made genocide a crime punishable by the international community
Warsaw Pact	1955	The communist response to NATO; created an alliance of Eastern European communist states
International Atomic Energy Treaty	1957	Regulates the use of atomic energy
Nuclear Non-Proliferation Treaty	1968	Made it illegal for states without atomic weapons to acquire them
Anti-Ballistic Missile Treaty	1972	Prevented the United States and the Soviet Union from developing antiballistic missiles
Camp David Accords	1978	A peace treaty between Egypt and Israel
Kyoto Protocol	2005	Regulates greenhouse emissions to reduce global warming

CHAPTER 6

International Organizations

Some international agreements create **international organizations,** which are institutions that set rules for nations and provide venues for diplomacy. There are two types of international organizations: **international governmental organizations** (IGOs) and **international nongovernmental organizations** (INGOs or, more commonly, NGOs). In recent years, **multinational corporations** (MNCs) have also had a significant impact on the international system.

IGOs and NGOs exist for a variety of reasons, such as controlling the proliferation of conventional and nuclear weapons, supervising trade, maintaining military alliances, ending world hunger, and fostering the spread of democracy and peace.

IMPORTANT INTERNATIONAL ORGANIZATIONS			
Name	**Type**	**Date Founded**	**Members as of 2006**
Amnesty International	NGO	1961	1.8 million members in 150 countries
European Union (EU)	IGO	1992	25 states, including the United Kingdom, Sweden, and Estonia
International Olympic Committee (IOC)	NGO	1894	115 individuals, who represent the IOC in their home countries
Organization of Petroleum Exporting Countries (OPEC)	IGO	1960	11 states, including Venezuela, Qatar, and Indonesia
Salvation Army	NGO	1878	Runs programs in more than 100 countries; has 3.5 million volunteers

IMPORTANT INTERNATIONAL ORGANIZATIONS (CONT'D)			
Name	**Type**	**Date Founded**	**Members as of 2006**
Save the Children	NGO	1932	Helps children in poverty around the world, including the United States and Nepal
United Nations (UN)	IGO	1946	191 states, including Burkina Faso, Denmark, the United States, and Jamaica
World Bank	IGO	1945	Offers loans to more than 100 states, including Cameroon and Senegal

INTERNATIONAL GOVERNMENTAL ORGANIZATIONS

IGOs form when governments make an agreement or band together. Only governments belong to IGOs, which are sometimes also known by the acronym IO (for *international organization*). The United Nations (UN), the North Atlantic Treaty Organization (NATO), the World Trade Organization (WTO), and the European Union (EU) are all examples of IGOs.

NONGOVERNMENTAL ORGANIZATIONS

Unlike governmental organizations, NGOs are made up of individuals, not businesses or governments. NGOs serve a variety of functions and represent numerous interests. Organizations that are not affiliated with governments but that nevertheless play an important role in international politics are called **nongovernmental actors.** Not all NGOs have a positive impact on global politics. Although Amnesty International has helped defend human rights, for example, the international terrorist organization al Qaeda has killed civilians in an effort to cripple economies and topple governments. Since the end of World War II, nongovernmental actors have become more important in the global arena.

CHAPTER 6

Know the NGO Lingo

People have devised a variety of acronyms to define specific types of NGOs, including:

INGO: international nongovernmental organization

BINGO: business-oriented nongovernmental organization

RINGO: religious-oriented nongovernmental organization

ENGO: environmental nongovernmental organization

GONGO: government-operated nongovernmental organization

QUANGO: quasi-autonomous nongovernmental organization

MULTINATIONAL CORPORATIONS

MNCs, or businesses that operate in more than one country, are another type of nongovernmental actor in the international system. Although MNCs are nongovernmental actors, they are not NGOs: As businesses, MNCs cannot be considered NGOs. Their primary aim is to make money. In the twenty-first century, MNCs dominate the global economy: According to the Coca-Cola corporation, for example, more than 70 million Coke products are consumed daily in Africa.

EXAMPLE: Some MNCs—such as Coca-Cola, Microsoft, and IBM, to name a few—are worth more than many small countries, which means that they have the power to be major players in international politics. In 2000, for instance, the Central Intelligence Agency declassified several documents that incriminated ITT, the International Telephone and Telegraph Company, of having funded rebels to topple the government of Chile and establish a new, more business-friendly government in the early 1970s.

War

War has been far too common in human history and thus is the central problem of international relations. Many political scientists and foreign policymakers view war as the continuation of politics: When diplomacy fails, some states decide to use force. Others see war as the result of a breakdown of the modern international system because so many of the rules of international institutions were designed to reduce conflict among states.

The Geneva Conventions

In 1864, several states created an international agreement that regulated acceptable behavior during war and armed conflicts. Since then, the Geneva Conventions have been amended in 1906, 1929, and 1949 as the nature of war and warfare has changed. The agreements prohibit torture, rape, genocide, mutilation, slavery, and other crimes against humanity. The conventions also state that prisoners of war must be treated humanely and that civilians may not be used as hostages.

CAUSES OF WAR

Political scientists have long debated the causes of war. These scholars have come up with the following list:

- **Human nature:** Humans are naturally violent and aggressive, making war inevitable.

- **Regime types:** Some regimes are more prone to waging war than others.

EXAMPLE: There has been extensive research on whether democracies are less likely to start wars than other regimes. Overall, it appears that democracies are less likely to fight other democracies, a phenomenon scholars refer to as the *democratic peace*. Democracies are, however, just as likely as other types of regimes to fight nondemocracies.

- **Ideology:** Some political beliefs favor war more than others. Some scholars blame fascism, for example, for World War II.

- **Religion:** Religious belief has driven many states to war, either to spread the faith or to eradicate heretics.

  EXAMPLE: During the early modern era, nearly every European country experienced numerous wars of religion as the Catholics sought to destroy the Protestants. The wars of religion culminated in the Thirty Years' War, which stretched from Spain and France to the eastern stretches of Germany during the seventeenth century. It was a brutal and horrific war, and the Catholics' failure to win the war marked the end of the major religious wars in Europe.

- **The global system:** Because the global system is anarchic, states must engage in war to protect themselves.

- **Economics and resources:** Disputes over resources often lead to war.

JUST-WAR THEORY

Debate has raged as long as wars have been fought as to whether a war can be morally just. Some prominent thinkers have proposed a **just-war theory,** which argues that wars should be fought for noble and worthwhile reasons. Just-war theorists also try to establish ethical rules for warfare. Of course, whether any war is justified is almost always a matter of debate. But most just-war theorists agree on some basic ideas:

- War must be the last option. All peaceful means to resolve the conflict must be exhausted before war breaks out.

- The cause of the war must be just (such as overturning aggression and righting a great wrong).

- The war must be winnable.

- The war's purpose must justify the cost in money and lives.

- The military must make every effort to prevent or limit civilian casualties.

"The Good War"

World War II is one of the few wars that nearly everyone believes was morally justified. Nazi Germany and Japan were dangerous regimes that committed atrocities against conquered peoples, and many nations felt that they needed to be stopped. For these reasons, some refer to World War II as "the good war." In contrast, the social and political turmoil caused by the Vietnam War was based, in part, on debate over whether that war was justified.

CHAPTER 6

TYPES OF WAR

Although all wars are violent, not all wars are the same. In fact, there are many different types of wars, which can be classified according to which people actually fight, the intensity of the conflict, and the extent of combatants' use of violence, among other factors.

Scholars generally describe five types of war:

1. Total war

2. Limited war

3. Guerrilla war

4. Civil war

5. Proxy war

Total War

A **total war** is a war in which combatants use every resource available to destroy the social fabric of the enemy. Total wars are highly destructive and are characterized by mass civilian casualties because winning a total war often requires combatants to break the people's will to continue fighting. World Wars I and II were total wars, marked by the complete destruction of the civilian economy and society in many countries, including France, Germany, the Soviet Union, Italy, Great Britain, and Japan.

Limited War

A **limited war** is a war fought primarily between professional armies to achieve specific political objectives without causing widespread destruction. Although the total of civilian casualties may be high, combatants do not seek to completely destroy the enemy's social and economic frameworks. The Persian Gulf War of 1990–1991 was a limited war in which the United States and its allies forcibly removed Iraqi troops from Kuwait.

Guerrilla War

A **guerrilla war** is a war in which one or both combatants use small, lightly armed militia units rather than professional, organized armies. Guerrilla fighters usually seek to topple their government, often enjoying the support of the people. These wars are often very long but also tend to be successful for the insurgents as evidenced by Mao Zedong's victory over Chiang Kai-shek in China in the 1940s, the Vietcong's victory over the United States in the Vietnam War, and the Mujahideen's victory over the Soviet Union in Afghanistan in the 1980s.

Civil War

A **civil war** is a war fought within a single country between or among different groups of citizens who want to control the government and do not recognize another group's right to rule. Civil wars are almost always total wars because each side feels compelled to destroy the enemy's political support base. Regional rifts, such as the American Civil War between the North and the South, characterize some civil wars, whereas other civil wars have been fought among ethnic rivals, religious rivals, and rival clans. Revolutions can spark civil wars as well.

Proxy War

A **proxy war** is a war fought by third parties rather than by the enemy states themselves. Many of the militarized conflicts during the Cold War, such as the Korean War and the Vietnam War, can be interpreted as proxy wars between the United States and the Soviet Union, neither of which wanted to fight each other directly.

CHAPTER 6

Categorizing Wars

A war can often be a limited war, a guerrilla war, and a civil war all at the same time. The Soviet invasion of Afghanistan in 1979 is a great example. The United States sent trainers, money, and weapons to Afghan rebels to fight against the invaders, making it a low-intensity, limited conflict from the U.S. point of view. The Afghan resistance mostly relied on guerrilla tactics. And the war split Afghanistan, so it was also a civil war.

INTERVENTION

Intervention is a fairly common way for a third-party state to get involved in a civil war or a war between two or more other states. A state intervenes when it sends troops, arms, money, or goods to help another state that is already at war. During the Cold War, the term *intervention* was used to describe one of the superpowers becoming involved in a smaller country's war (often a developing country).

But states sometimes intervene in order to bring peace. This type of intervention occurs when a country (or countries) sends military forces into another state to act as peacekeepers or to block other forces from attacking. Sometimes these interventions are organized or conducted by the United Nations or another international governmental organization.

EXAMPLE: The United States, along with other NATO nations, sent troops into the former Yugoslavia on a number of occasions to protect people from war. A successful example of this peaceful intervention occurred during the 1999 U.S. bombing campaign in Kosovo, which helped stop a slaughter of Kosovars by attacking Serbs. A less successful example was the U.S. intervention in Somalia in the early 1990s, an attempt to provide humanitarian aid that ultimately achieved little at the cost of American lives. This failed intervention culminated in the Battle of Mogadishu (dramatized in the movie *Black Hawk Down* [2001]) October 3–4, 1993, which killed eighteen Americans and as many as a thousand Somalis.

Revolution

A **revolution** is any fundamental change in the social or political aspects of a state. Most revolutions are political, occurring when the citizens of a country try to oust the existing government and replace it with a new one. Political revolutions tend to be tumultuous, violent events. There is no clear-cut explanation as to why people revolt, but scholars believe that some or all of the following factors lead to revolution:

- **Injustice:** Aristotle argued that the cause of revolution was the perception of injustice. If the underclasses feel that they are being treated unjustly, they will revolt.

- **Relative deprivation:** Some scholars have argued that revolutions occur after a period of good times has ended. The citizens begin to expect a higher quality of life and feel cheated when they perceive a stagnation or decline in the quality of their lives.

- **State of the government:** Revolutions are more likely to happen in countries with corrupt governments. If citizens believe in the efficacy of their government, then revolution is unlikely. But if a regime appears to exist solely to enrich the rulers, then revolution is more likely.

- **The military:** As the strongest power in most states, the military frequently determines whether a revolution will occur and be successful. If the military backs the government, then revolution is unlikely. A turning point in many revolutions occurs when soldiers decide to stop obeying the government and decide to fight alongside the revolutionaries.

CHAPTER 6

REVOLUTIONS IN HISTORY

Although people have always rebelled against their rulers and governments, the modern area witnessed many significant revolutions. Since the sixteenth century, most revolutions have been attempts to overthrow traditional regimes in the name of liberty. In the twentieth century alone, there were important revolutions in Russia, China, Egypt, and parts of communist Eastern Europe, as well as countless others in smaller countries. Revolutions, and countering revolutions, were a driving force of foreign policy in the twentieth century. However, three revolutions in particular have served as models for most of the world's revolutions in the nineteenth and twentieth centuries:

- **American Revolution** (1776–1783): Leaders of the American Revolution overthrew British colonial rule to establish an independent republic. These colonial leaders considered the revolution to be a necessary evil and restricted the use of violence. Although the revolution affected the lives of most Americans, there was little social upheaval.

- **French Revolution** (1788–1799): The French Revolution began much as the American Revolution had but quickly turned violent. Tens of thousands of French citizens were executed during Maximilian Robespierre's so-called Reign of Terror. Order was restored only when Napoleon Bonaparte seized control of the government.

- **Russian Revolution** (1917): Russian revolutionaries sought both the removal of the monarchy and the complete restructuring of civil society in accordance with Vladimir Lenin's version of communism. The second phase of the Russian Revolution served as the model for dozens of other communist revolutions.

Fostering Revolution

Some nations have encouraged and supported revolutions in other countries as a foreign policy tool. For most of its existence, the Soviet Union promoted communist parties and revolutions around the world, most notoriously through the Comintern. Similarly, the United States fostered revolutions in such places as Iraq, Iran, Guatemala, and Nicaragua.

MAJOR REVOLUTIONS IN MODERN HISTORY			
Revolution	**Place**	**Dates**	**Major Impact**
English Civil War	England	1642–1653	Set the stage for limited monarchy, and eventually democracy, in England
Glorious Revolution	England	1688	Permanently ended absolute monarchy in England
American Revolution	United States	1775–1783	Created the first modern democratic state
French Revolution	France	1789–1799	Destroyed the old French monarchy, led to the creation of the French nation-state, and promoted nationalism around Europe
Haitian Revolution	Haiti	1804	Created the first free black republic
French Revolution of 1830	France	1830	Permanently ended French monarchy
Mexican Revolution	Mexico	1910	Overthrew the dictator Porfirio Díaz and created the modern Mexican state
Russian Revolution	Russia	1917	Ended czarist rule in Russia and created the first communist state
Spanish Revolution	Spain	1936	Turned Spain into a fascist state
Chinese Civil War	China	1949	Turned China into a communist state

CHAPTER 6

MAJOR REVOLUTIONS IN MODERN HISTORY (CONT'D)			
Revolution	**Place**	**Dates**	**Major Impact**
Algerian War of Independence	Algeria	1954–1962	Ended French imperial control of Algeria
Cuban Revolution	Cuba	1959	Overthrew Batista and created a communist regime
Iranian Revolution	Iran	1979	Overthrew the shah and created an Islamic regime
Nicaraguan Revolution	Nicaragua	1979	Overthrew the despotic regime and brought Marxist Sandinistas to power
Revolutions of 1989	Eastern Europe	1989	Ended Soviet and communist rule of many Eastern European states

SUCCESS AND FAILURE

Revolutions are extremely difficult to achieve. For a revolution to succeed, many people must agree that the government needs to be overthrown, and these people must be willing to put themselves in danger and prepare for the possibility of civil war. Moreover, revolutions usually fail. For example, in Europe in 1848, democratic ideas and the free market spawned a series of revolutions across the continent. Most of them failed miserably, and perhaps the main impact of the revolutions of 1848 was the strengthening of authoritarian rule.

The Industrial Revolution

Not all revolutions are political. A *social revolution* is a revolution that transforms society or the economy without drastically altering the existing political system. The Industrial Revolution of the late eighteenth and early nineteenth centuries had a major impact on every country in the world. Beginning around 1780 in England, industry started to replace agriculture, and machinery started to replace manual labor. By the mid-nineteenth century, new forms of production and transportation—including the invention of the steam engine, mechanical typesetting, and movies—had fundamentally altered the modern world. Consequently, the lives of Europeans changed drastically within just a couple of decades.

Terrorism

Terrorism is the use of violence (often against civilian targets) to instill fear, generate publicity, and sometimes destabilize governments. Generally speaking, small groups fighting against powerful states practice terrorism, but governments also have the ability to practice terrorism. Throughout history, terrorism has taken many forms. Just in the last two centuries, for example, terrorism has been used by Russian nihilists, nationalists in Israel, Nazi forces, environmentalists worldwide, left-wing guerrillas in Europe, discontented radicals in the United States, Latin American death squads, and Islamic fundamentalists. Terrorism is not tied to any one particular ideology or group.

TYPES OF TERRORISM

Scholars generally classify terrorism into two types: terrorism practiced by governments and terrorism practiced by groups not affiliated with a government. **Ideological terrorism** aims to promote a particular belief system through acts of violence; it may be practiced by both governments and groups.

TYPES OF TERRORISM

Terrorism Practiced by Governments

- **State terrorism:** A government commits acts of terror against its own citizens.

- **International terrorism** (also known as **state-sponsored terrorism**): A government supplies and trains terrorists to make attacks in other countries.

Terrorism Practiced by Groups

- **Antistate terrorism:** Any terrorist act not committed by a government

- **Domestic terrorism:** A group with no ties to another country or government commits terrorist acts within its own country.

Some types of terrorism fit into more than one of these categories. Suicide bombings in Israel, for example, are ideological (promoting a Palestinian state and sometimes also promoting Islamic fundamentalism), state-sponsored (a number of Arab governments fund the bombers), and domestic (many are carried out by Arabs living in Israel).

Guerrillas Versus Terrorists

Although guerrillas have been known to practice terrorism, guerrillas are not terrorists. Guerrillas fight against their governments, particularly against the military, in order to provoke a regime change. Terrorists, in contrast, target civilians and members of the military in order to create a social and political crisis of international proportions. Of course, those fighting a guerrilla group might label their opponents terrorists, and some terrorists may see themselves as guerrillas.

THE PURPOSE OF TERRORISM

Terrorist acts ultimately aim to undermine governments and disrupt societies. Many terrorists are young, frustrated men who feel that they have been treated unjustly. Sometimes terrorists try to destabilize a government directly, via assassinations, kidnappings, and the bombing of government buildings. Terrorists can also work to undermine governments indirectly by showing people that their leaders are too weak to prevent the attacks and that an active resistance movement exists. Sometimes, terrorists attack in order to provoke a strong response from the government, hoping that the response will alienate more people from the government and foster even more political discord.

> *EXAMPLE:* Many scholars and political analysts have argued that President George W. Bush played into al Qaeda's hands by passing the Patriot Act in 2001 and by invading Iraq in 2003. The Patriot Act gave the federal government more power to detain and question suspected terrorists—often without trial—and to monitor suspicious activity. The Iraq War, meanwhile, deeply divided Americans when it became clear that Saddam Hussein had no connection with al Qaeda and was not harboring weapons of mass destruction. The federal government's suspension of some civil liberties along with the specter of deceit has shattered much of the unity Americans felt in the wake of the September 11th terrorist attacks.

CHAPTER 6

Sample Test Questions

1. Define international system.

2. In what ways do realism and liberalism differ?

3. What are the two major revolutions that have inspired other revolutionaries in the modern era?

4. True or false: Religious groups always practice terrorism.

5. True or false: A total war is also usually a guerrilla war.

6. Since the end of the Cold War, some foreign affairs experts believe that the world has moved toward a _____ system.

    A. bipolar
    B. unipolar
    C. regional
    D. monetary

7. Which of the following is generally not considered to be a cause of war?

    A. God's will
    B. Human nature
    C. Economics
    D. The international system

8. Which of the following is *not* a type of nongovernmental actor?

    A. MNC
    B. NGO
    C. GDP
    D. IO

9. What is international law?

    A. A binding regulations on states
    B. A combination of tradition, custom, and international agreements that sometimes limit the behavior of states
    C. Any law passed by a country that deals with international relations
    D. A law of physics that applies in all places

10. How does domestic terrorism differ from state-sponsored terrorism?

    A. Domestic terrorism is sponsored by another government.
    B. State-sponsored terrorism is only used against military targets.
    C. Domestic terrorism is only used against military targets.
    D. Domestic terrorism has no ties to other governments.

ANSWERS

1. The international system is the set of rules by which states relate to one another. Most of these rules arise from tradition and custom, but states can break them at times. Each state is sovereign.

2. Although both realism and liberalism are predicated on the assumption that the world is an anarchic place, realism emphasizes the desire of states to increase their military power relative to other states, whereas liberalism stresses the importance of economic engagement and the role of international institutions.

3. The American and French Revolutions have served as models for many modern revolutions.

4. False

5. False

6. B

7. A

8. C

9. B

10. D

CHAPTER 6

Suggested Reading

- Arendt, Hannah. *On Revolution.* New York: Penguin Classics, 1991.

Arendt's philosophical descriptions of some of history's greatest revolutions are dramatic and profound.

- Aron, Raymond. *The Century of Total War.* Lanham, Md.: University Press of America, 1985.

Aron, an extremely influential thinker in political science, explores the causes and consequences of war in the bloodiest century in history.

- Axelrod, Robert. *The Evolution of Cooperation.* New York: Basic Books, 1984.

Axelrod ran an experiment in which computer programs competed with one another by cooperating or defecting. He found that cooperation could arise in an anarchic environment because programs that cooperated often benefited more than those that did not.

- Kegley, Charles W., Jr., ed. *International Terrorism: Characteristics, Causes, Controls.* New York: St. Martin's Press, 1990.

Numerous scholars tackle the thorny problem of terrorism.

- Keohane, Robert, and Joseph S. Nye. *Power and Interdependence.* 2nd ed. Glencoe, Ill.: Scott Foresman, 1989.

The founding book of complex interdependence theory.

- Morgenthau, Hans J. *Politics Among Nations: The Struggle for Power and Peace.* 5th ed. New York: McGraw-Hill, 1992.

A very influential American realist's major work. Morgenthau argues that states must pursue power in order to protect their national interests.

- Rosecrance, Richard. *Rise of the Trading State.* New York: Basic Books, 1986.

A historical approach to the complex interdependence theory.

- Skocpol, Theda. *States and Social Revolutions: A Comparative Analysis of France, Russia, and China.* New York: Cambridge University Press, 1979.

Skocpol is one of the key figures in the "return to the state" movement. In this classic of comparative politics, she looks at why some revolutions succeed and others fail.

- Waltz, Kenneth. *Man, the State, and War: A Theoretical Analysis.* New York: Columbia University Press, 1965.

What causes war? Waltz examines three possibilities and settles on the international system as the root cause.

- Walzer, Michael. *Just and Unjust War: A Moral Argument with Historical Illustrations.* 3rd ed. New York: Basic Books, 2000.

A leading contemporary philosopher takes up the question of the morality of war.

CHAPTER 6

Useful Websites

- http://nsi.org/terrorism.html

Sponsored by the National Security Institute, this website contains facts about terrorism, as well as gives tips about how to avoid and prevent it.

- www.cscs.umich.edu/Software/CC/ECHome.html

A website devoted to Robert Axelrod's cooperation project and book *The Evolution of Cooperation*.

- www.iiss.org

The website of the Institute for Strategic Studies, a watchdog organization for political-military conflicts around the world.

- www.isn.ethz.ch

The International Relations and Security Network website contains a great deal of information and many links to information about international security issues.

- www.terrorism.net

A comprehensive website for those interested in knowing more about terrorism and counterterrorism.

- www.un.org

The website of the United Nations.

- www.worldviewwest.com

A resource for students and teachers interested in international affairs and foreign policy.

APPENDIX

A+ Student Essays

Politics and Political Ideologies

Which political ideology had the greatest impact and influence in the twentieth century? Which ideology do you believe will have the greatest impact in the twenty-first century? Use specific examples to support your argument.

Despite the spread of fascism and communism during the first half of the twentieth century, liberalism had the greatest impact in the twentieth century. In fact, liberalism has triumphed over both fascism and communism and has proven to be the most effective method for maintaining political stability and fostering economic prosperity. Because democracy and capitalism give the greatest degree of political power to individuals, liberalism will continue to flourish in the twenty-first century.

The first decades of the twentieth century witnessed the collapse of Old World monarchies in Europe, Russia, and much of Asia. In the aftermath of World War I, war-torn societies turned to alternative systems of government. Many Europeans and Asians believed that fascism and socialist communism were viable alternatives to monarchy. Fascism, for example, took root in Italy, Spain, and Germany—the countries perhaps hardest hit by the global depression—and people looked to anyone who offered immediate solutions to their poverty. Politicians such as Benito Mussolini in Italy, Francisco Franco in Spain, and Adolf Hitler in

Germany promised food, jobs, prosperity, and national strength. Fascism also imbued the people with a sense of individual and national pride. It soon became apparent, however, that fascism and totalitarianism went hand in hand, as Mussolini, Franco, and Hitler quickly became dictators. Each of these men brutalized his people to unprecedented degrees, and Hitler alone systematically killed more than six million Jews, homosexuals, and handicapped people. Hitler's brutality and zeal for territorial expansion eventually led to World War II in Europe, in which liberal democracy and communism ultimately triumphed.

Like fascism, communism also seemed like a better alternative to monarchy, especially because socialists and communists championed the rights of the working classes, the downtrodden, and those without property. Communism, in theory, was the people's government. After World War II, the alliance among the United States, France, and Great Britain in the democratic West and communist Russia and China quickly disintegrated into the Cold War, as proponents of the two ideologies vied for global influence. Both the United States and the Soviet Union tried to spread their ideologies and establish loyal puppet governments in strategic regions around the world. But whereas the Western capitalist economies flourished under democratic governments, the people living under communist regimes in the Soviet Union and China faced greater financial hardship and violence. Just as the fascists had murdered millions of civilians, so too did the communist dictators Joseph Stalin and Mao Zedong, each of whom killed between 20 million and 30 million of his own people through reigns of terror and unsound economic policies. These policies led to the collapse of the Soviet Union in the early 1990s, at a time when the American economy and democracy had never been stronger. China too quietly renounced communism in the last decade of the twentieth century and embraced capitalism.

Democracy triumphed over monarchy, fascism, and communism in the last century because it empowers the individual both politically and economically. Unlike other systems of government, democracies give the people direct control over their governments and financial institutions and maximize individual liberty in the marketplace. As a result, democracies are usually the most politically stable and prosperous countries in the world. For these reasons, democracy will undoubtedly continue to flourish in the twenty-first century.

Political Economy

> You have been named the absolute ruler of your own country. Which type of economy would you want your country to have, and why? What steps would you take to help balance the economy? Use specific examples to support your argument.

If I were the absolute ruler of my own country, I would want to create and maintain a capitalist economy. As I will demonstrate, command economies have proven highly ineffective. At the same time, however, I would enact certain measures to temper the income inequality inherent to capitalist economies.

Nearly every twentieth-century command economy has failed because central planners cannot possibly anticipate every facet of an economy. Countries with command economies have often suffered severe commodity shortages and hyperinflation as demand for the few available goods skyrockets. Black markets inevitably emerge to compensate for the failures of the central planners. In fact, given enough time, most command economies collapse completely, as they did in the Soviet Union in 1990 and North Korea in the mid-1990s. Recognizing the inherent failures of this system and fearful of their own economic collapse, authorities in communist China have been instituting economic reforms since the 1980s, starting with the agricultural sector and eventually privatizing state-run businesses in the 1990s. The Chinese actively seek foreign direct investment in Chinese business ventures, and Chinese legislators just recently legalized the ownership of private property, which strictly violates traditional communist economic philosophy. China's willingness to protect people's private property and encourage foreign investment in its increasingly free-market economy is a testament to the triumph of capitalism over centrally planned economies.

Capitalism has its evils too, however, which is why I would enact a number of policies in my country to temper the free market. The greatest threat capitalism poses is excessive income inequality, when the wealthy control a grossly disproportionate share of the national wealth. Wealth in and of itself is not a social evil, but too much income inequality can place undue hardship on the people in the poorer brackets of society, leading to recession, depression, or even social unrest. To reduce income inequality, I would enact a progressive, graduated income tax, which would relieve the tax burden on poorer people, in order to redistribute some of my country's economic goods. Tax credits, such as an earned income tax credit, would also be useful in keeping more money in the hands of those who earned it and need it the most. Sound monetary policies—adjusting interest rates to control the national money supply, for instance—would also help keep inflation and unemployment in check.

In addition, I would regulate some sectors of the economy in order to restrain the marketplace. Assuming that agriculture played a key role in the national economy, I would follow the American and European models by subsidizing farming to keep production within certain levels and to prevent food surpluses and shortages. I would also set some limits on the banking and financial sectors to prevent unsound speculation, which has been partially responsible for recessions and depressions in the past. Finally, I would institute some form of corporate codeterminism, forcing large companies to seat a sizable number of blue-collar representatives on their governing boards. Giving employees a greater say in corporate policy increases communication between management and workers, and this practice has been known to reduce labor related conflicts in Western European countries.

Even though I would rely on the so-called invisible hand of the marketplace instead of the central planners involved in command economies, my country would not be purely capitalist. Instead, it would rely on a free market checked only with sound fiscal and monetary policies, as well as appropriate regulation, in order to reduce excessive unequal distribution of wealth and to maintain social stability.

Political Culture and Public Opinion

A key component of political culture is citizenship. Americans today usually interpret citizenship as the natural extension of our liberal democratic ideology. But our modern conception of citizenship differs drastically from that of previous generations. How has the concept of citizenship changed throughout American history? Use specific examples to support your argument.

Many people assume that the privilege of citizenship in the United States represents the culmination of more than 200 years of democratic rule. Such an assumption, however, is dangerously misleading. If we casually assume that the United States has granted citizenship to people in accordance with the principles of democratic government, we run the risk of ignoring Americans in the past who have been unjustly denied citizenship. In fact, exploring the concept of citizenship in the United States demonstrates that citizenship is more of a testament to economic and political self-interest than to democratic ideals.

Millions of people throughout the world look to the United States as the epitome of egalitarianism and acceptance. Because citizenship stems from a combination of the French model *jus soli* (citizenship based on birthplace) and the German model *jus sanguines* (citizenship based on blood), America is often seen as a place where anyone from any ethnicity can live equally under the law. American cities teem with citizens from all ethnic backgrounds, and American society celebrates multicultural, hyphenated identities. Naturalization is relatively easy: It requires just a five-year residency, proficiency in the English language, and basic knowledge of American government and history. In fact, America grants permanent resident status to more immigrants than any other nation in the world. The United States, then, seems to be a perfectly egalitarian state that guarantees rights to anyone interested in applying for citizenship, open to all without prejudices toward outsiders.

In reality, however, this utopian nation does not exist, even in America. A close examination of the history of American citizenship tells a much different story. Although prosperous whites have had the privilege of citizenship since long before the Declaration of Independence was drafted, poor whites, women, blacks, Native Americans, and Asians were excluded from voting and denied full citizenship status throughout much of American history. Blacks were not granted citizenship rights until the passage of the Thirteenth, Fourteenth, and Fifteenth Amendments, nearly 100 years after Independence. Even then, black Americans faced intense racial and political discrimination. Native Americans were likewise prohibited from citizenship until they had proven their "worth" in defending the United States during World War I, and Asian immigrants were banned from citizenship until China fought with the United States against the Japanese during World War II. In these cases, the right to naturalize was extended only as a method of payment for services provided, not as a noble extension of equality. None of these policies adheres to the democratic ideology of equality in government; instead, they indicate a concept of citizenship based on national self-interest. The government grants citizenship when it feels it has something to gain.

Societies are generally more exclusive than inclusive. The United States itself, with its steadfast Constitution, inalienable rights, and unparalleled diversity, has arbitrarily used its power to allocate citizenship to those it feels are good enough. State interests and motivations alone, and not democratic ideology, determine which inhabitants become citizens and when. In the words of sociologist and philosopher Max Weber, "Not ideas, but interests—material and ideal—directly govern men's conduct."

International Politics

Is realism still a valid lens through which to analyze international relations? Why or why not? Use specific examples to support your argument.

Despite increased globalization and international trade, as well as the growing reliance on international institutions to resolve disputes peacefully, realism is still an effective tool for analyzing international relations. In fact, realism is the only appropriate lens through which to examine the international relations in some regions of the world. Nowhere is realism more relevant, for example, than in East Asia.

Burdened with legacies of numerous civil wars, invasions, and military occupations over the last century, East Asia retains an atmosphere of fear and mutual distrust. This atmosphere is particularly acute in the relationship between North Korea and its neighbors and the United States, a key military and economic actor in the region. Fearful of an American invasion, North Korea currently has nuclear weapons and one of the largest standing armies in the world. Distrust and paranoia after World War II and the Korean War have prompted South Korea and Japan to seek military protection. These two countries have not developed nuclear weapons of their own due to their military alliances with and assurances of defense from the United States. China, nominally Pyongyang's only ally in the region, is also nervous about a nuclear North Korea but hopes to prevent the collapse of its communist neighbor in order to keep a buffer between itself and the American-backed South Korea. Mutual mistrust and fear have prompted many foreign policy analysts to claim that the Cold War continues on the Korean Peninsula.

The distrust between China and Japan results in territorial disputes and chilly relations, despite the lucrative trade between the two countries. China plays on the anti-Japanese sentiments of the Chinese people, who remember Japan's brutal occupation of China in the 1930s and 1940s. The neo-nationalist movement in Japan that seeks to gloss over Japanese atrocities during the war also fuels Chinese anger. Both countries also claim a number of small islands off the coast of Taiwan, which lie in prime fishing waters and serve as powerful symbols of Chinese and Japanese territorial integrity. Having fought and lost two wars against the Japanese in the twentieth century, China fears that Japan may one day invade China again and has therefore sought to strengthen itself militarily. A growing threat from China, in turn, has prompted many Japanese politicians to publicly debate amending the Japanese constitution, which currently forbids the use of the Japanese military. Even though the two countries engage in hundreds of billions of dollars in annual trade, a liberalist lens would fail to capture the fear and distrust Japan and China have of and for each other.

The feud between Japan and China, however, is merely part of a much larger feud developing between China and the United States. Over the past decade, Beijing and Washington have become engaged in a developing arms race over Taiwan. China resents Taiwan's de facto claim of independence from the mainland as well as America's unwavering support for the small island power. Taiwan, a capitalist democracy, has threatened to formally break away from Beijing on numerous occasions, despite China's threat to invade the island if it ever actually did break away. Even though the United States does not officially recognize Taiwan as an independent country, it has nevertheless promised to defend Taiwan against Chinese military aggression. The United States has also consistently sold weapons and military equipment to the Taiwanese so that the Taiwanese may better defend themselves and "restore the balance of power" between Beijing and Taipei. American assistance to Taiwan has prompted China to increase its own military spending to combat the Taiwanese advantage. China and the United States are the world's two greatest trading partners, but given China's unyielding stance on Taiwan, some foreign policy analysts predict that the Sino-American arms race will continue until military confrontation erupts.

Since the end of the Cold War, trade has replaced fear as the common international currency. International institutions, such as the World Trade Organization, the United Nations, the World Bank, and the International Monetary Fund, have all worked steadily for peace, stability, and development. Nevertheless, fear and mutual distrust still dominate policymaking in some regions of the world—and realisms is simply the best tool with which to analyze international relations marked by such characteristics.

Glossary

A

absentee ballot: A ballot, usually sent in the mail, that allows those who cannot go to their precinct on election day to vote.

absolutism: The belief that the government should have all the power and be able to do whatever it wants.

acquisitive model: A view of bureaucracies that argues agency heads seek to expand the size, budget, and power of their agency.

actual malice: Knowingly printing falsehoods in order to harm a person's reputation.

administrative adjudication: The bureaucratic function of settling disputes by relying on rules and precedents.

affirm: An action by the Supreme Court to uphold a ruling by a lower court; that ruling is now the legally binding one.

affirmative action: Measures to give minorities special consideration for hiring, school admission, and so on, designed to overcome past discrimination.

agency capture: The gaining of control (direct or indirect) over a government regulatory agency by the industry it regulates.

agency representation: A type of representation in which the representative is seen as an agent, acting on behalf of the district, who is held accountable if he or she does not do as the constituents wish.

agenda-setting: The power of the media to determine which issues will be discussed and debated.

amendment: A change to the Constitution.

American conservatism: The belief that freedom trumps all other political considerations; the government should play a small role in people's lives.

American exceptionalism: The view that the United States is different from other countries.

American liberalism: The belief that the government should promote equality in politics and economics.

Americans with Disabilities Act: The major law banning discrimination against the disabled, it requires employers to make all reasonable accommodations to disabled workers; it passed in 1990.

amicus curiae brief: Literally, a "friend of the court" brief. A brief submitted to the court by a group not involved in the case; it presents further arguments for one side in the case.

anarchism: The belief that all governments are repressive and should be destroyed.

appellate jurisdiction: The authority to review cases heard by lower courts.

appointment power: The president's power to appoint people to key federal offices.

appropriation: The act of Congress formally specifying the amount of authorized money that an agency can spend.

Articles of Confederation: America's first national constitution, which loosely bound the states under a weak national Congress.

attack journalism: Journalism that aims to undermine political leaders.

Australian ballot: A ballot printed by the government that allows voting to be secret.

authoritarian regime: A government that can do whatever it wants, without limits.

authority: The ability of the government to exercise power without resorting to violence.

authorization: A formal declaration by a congressional committee that a certain amount of money is available to an agency.

autocracy: A regime in which the government holds all the power.

B

bad-tendency rule: A rule to judge if speech can be limited: If the speech could lead to some sort of "evil," it can be prohibited.

Bakke **case:** This Supreme Court Case decided in 1978 that affirmative action is legal as long as race is not the only factor considered.

balanced budget: When a government spends exactly as much as it takes in.

bicameral legislature: A legislature with two houses.

bilateral: A state acting in cooperation with another state.

bill: A proposed law or policy.

bill of attainder: A bill passed by the legislature that declares a person guilty of a crime.

Bill of Rights: The first ten amendments to the Constitution, which safeguard some specific rights of the American people and the states.

Bipartisan Campaign Finance Reform Act: A law passed in 2002 that banned soft money, put limits on issue advertising, and increased the amount people can donate to candidates; also called the *McCain-Feingold bill.*

bipolar system: An international system characterized by two superpowers that roughly balance each other.

blanket primary: A primary in which voters can choose candidates from more than one party; declared unconstitutional by the Supreme Court.

block grant: A grant-in-aid with few restrictions or rules about how it can be spent.

blog: A weblog on the Internet; the thoughts and opinions of a person or group posted online.

brief: A document submitted to a court that presents one side's argument in a case.

broadcast media: Media that is distributed over the airwaves.

Brown v. Board of Education of Topeka, Kansas: Supreme Court case that ended segregation and declared "separate but equal" to be unconstitutional.

bundling: The practice of lumping campaign donations from several donors together.

bureaucracy: An administrative way of organizing large numbers of people to work together; usually relies on specialization, hierarchy, and standard operating procedure.

buying power: One's ability to purchase things; it is undermined by inflation.

C

cabinet: A group, composed of the heads of federal departments and key agencies, that advises the president.

caesaropapism: The belief that the powers of church and state should be united in one person.

candidate-centered politics: Campaigns and politics that focus on the candidates, not party labels.

case law: The collection of court decisions that shape law.

casework: Work done by a member of Congress or his or her staff on behalf of constituents.

categorical grants: Money given for a specific purpose that comes with restrictions concerning how the money should be spent. There are two types of categorical grants: project grants and formula grants.

caucus: A gathering of political leaders to make decisions, such as which candidate to nominate for an office; set policy; and plot strategy.

census: Counting the population to determine representation in the House of Representatives; the constitution mandates one every ten years.

central bank: The institution with the power to implement monetary policy.

centralization: the process by which law- and policymaking becomes centrally located.

centrally planned economy: An economy where all decisions are made by the government.

charter: A document issued by state government granting certain powers and responsibilities to a local government.

checks and balances: The ability of different branches of government to stop each other from acting; designed to prevent one branch from gaining too much power.

chief of state: The ceremonial head of government; in the United States, the president serves as chief of state.

citizen: A legal member of a political unit.

civic education: Education geared toward training the young to be good citizens.

civil liberties: Individual freedoms that the government cannot take away, including free speech, freedom of religion, and the rights of the accused.

civil rights: The rights of equality under the law.

Civil Rights Act of 1964: The major civil rights legislation in the modern era, the Civil Rights Act banned discrimination and segregation in public accommodations.

Civil Rights Cases: Supreme Court decision in 1883 that said the Fourteenth Amendment only made discrimination by government illegal; private citizens could do as they pleased.

civil service: Government employees hired and promoted based on merit, not political connections.

Civil Service Commission: The first federal personnel agency.

Civil Service Reform Act of 1883: Law that established the federal civil service; also known as the *Pendleton Act.*

Civil Service Reform Act of 1978: Law that updated and reformed the civil service.

civil society: The network of community relationships that builds social capital.

civil war: A war fought within a single country between or among different groups of citizens who want to control the government and do not recognize another group's right to rule.

classical conservatism: A view that arose in opposition to classical liberalism; it claimed that tradition was very valuable, human reason limited, and stability essential.

classical liberalism: A view that arose in the early modern era in Europe; it argues for the value of the individual, the necessity for freedom, the importance of rationalism, and the value of the free market.

clear-and-present danger: A limit on free speech stipulating that speech that constitutes a "clear and present danger" can be banned.

closed primary: A primary in which the voter must belong to the party in which he or she participates.

closed rule: A rule on a bill, issued by the House Rules Committee, which limits or bans amendments during floor debate.

cloture: A motion to end debate in the Senate, it must be approved by sixty votes.

codetermination: A policy used in some states with strong social democratic parties that forces large corporations to have substantial representation from the workers on the board of directors

command economy: An economy where all decisions are made by the government.

commerce clause: A clause in Article I, Section 8, of the U.S. Constitution that grants Congress the power to regulate interstate commerce.

common-carrier role: The media's role as an intermediary between the people and the government.

common law: A system of law, originally from England, in which previous decisions guide judges in interpreting the law.

communism: An extreme form of socialism that advocates violent revolution to create a socialist state.

comparative politics: An academic discipline that compares states in order to understand how they work.

concurrent powers: Powers exercised simultaneously by the states and the federal government.

concurring opinion: An opinion issued by a judge who votes with the winning side but disagrees with the majority or plurality opinion.

confederacy: A loose relationship among a number of smaller political units.

confederate system: A system of government with a very weak central government and strong states.

conformism: A tendency for people to act the same way, watch the same television programs, read the same books, and so on.

constituency: The people in a district represented by a legislator.

constitution: A set of rules that govern how power will be distributed and used legitimately in a state.

constitutional democracy: A type of government characterized by limitations on government power spelled out in a constitution.

constitutional government: A regime in which the use of power is limited by law.

constitutional powers: Powers of the president granted explicitly by the Constitution.

continuing resolution: A measure passed by Congress that temporarily funds an agency while Congress completes its budget.

conventional participation: Political participation in activities deemed appropriate by most; includes voting, donating to a campaign, and writing letters to officeholders.

convention delegate: A party member or official who goes to the national convention to vote for the party's presidential nominee and to ratify the party's platform.

cooperative federalism: A term used to describe federalism for most of the twentieth century (and into the twenty-first), where the federal government and the states work closely together and are intertwined; also known as *marble-cake federalism.*

corrupt practices acts: A series of laws in the early twentieth century that were the first attempts to regulate campaign finance.

credentials committee: Party officials who decide which delegates may participate in the national convention.

critical election: An election that marks the advent of a realignment.

D

dealignment: The loosening of party ties as more voters see themselves as independents.

decision: A document issued by the court stating who wins the case.

Declaration of Independence: The document written by Thomas Jefferson in 1776 that broke the colonies away from British rule.

de facto segregation: Segregation that exists due to economic and residential patterns, not because of law.

defamation of character: Unfairly hurting a person's reputation.

deficit spending: When a government intentionally spends more money than it takes in.

de jure segregation: Segregation imposed by law.

delegated powers: Powers granted by Congress to help the president fulfill his duties.

demand-side economics: An approach to economic policy that stresses stimulation of demand by putting more money in the hands of consumers.

democracy: Rule by the people.

democratic socialism: A peaceful form of socialism that works within democratic governments to attain socialism gradually.

demosclerosis: The inability of the U.S. government to get anything significant done because interest groups block all major change.

denial of power: Declaring that a certain person or group does not have a particular power.

depression: A severe economic downturn that lasts a long time; more serious than a recession.

deregulation: The repeal or reduction of regulations in order to boost efficiency, increase competitiveness, and benefit consumers.

deterrence: Threatening to use military force to prevent another state from taking a particular course of action.

GLOSSARY

devolution: The process of the national government giving responsibilities and powers to state, local, or regional governments.

dictatorship: An absolute government in which one person holds all the power and uses it for his or her own self-interest.

diplomacy: The act of negotiating and dealing with other nations in the world, trying to achieve goals without force.

direct democracy: A government in which the people come together to vote on all important issues.

discharge petition: A measure in the House that forces a bill out of a committee for consideration by the whole House.

dissenting opinion: A court opinion written by the losing side that explains why it disagrees with the decision.

diversity: A mix of different cultural and religious traditions and values.

divided government: A situation in which one party controls the presidency, while the other controls at least one house of Congress.

divine right theory of kingship: The view that the monarch is chosen by God to rule with absolute power over a country.

division of labor: The practice of dividing a job into smaller component parts and assigning one person or group to do each part.

dual federalism: A term to describe federalism through most of the nineteenth century, where the federal and state governments each had their own issue areas, which rarely overlapped; also known as *layer-cake federalism*.

due process clause: Part of the Fourteenth Amendment, which declares that no person can be deprived of life, liberty, or property without due process of law.

duopoly: A term to describe the overwhelming power of the two major parties in American politics.

E

Earned Income Tax Credit: A federal welfare program that refunds all or part of a poor family's social security tax.

economic aid: Assistance to other countries designed to help the recipient's economy.

economic group: An interest group that seeks material benefits for its members.

economic growth: The expansion of the economy, leading to the creation of more jobs and more wealth.

effective tax rate: The actual percentage of one's income that one pays in taxes, after deductions and tax credits.

elastic clause: Clause in Article I, Section 8, of the Constitution that says the Congress has the power to do anything that is necessary and proper in order to carry out its explicit powers; also called the *necessary and proper clause.*

elector: A member of the Electoral College.

Electoral College: The body that elects the president of the United States; composed of electors from each state equal to that state's representation in Congress; a candidate must get a majority of electoral votes to win.

elitism/elite theory: The view that a small capable group should rule over the rest.

emergency powers: Inherent powers exercised by the president to deal with emergencies.

empire: A state that governs more than one national group, usually as a result of conquest.

enabling legislation: A law passed by Congress that lays out the general purposes and powers of an agency but grants the agency the power to determine the details of how it implements policy.

entitlement program: A program under which the federal government is obligated to pay a specified benefit to people who meet certain requirements.

enumerated powers: The powers specifically given to Congress in Article I, Section 8, of the Constitution.

environmental impact statement: A statement that must be prepared by the federal government prior to acting that describes how the environment will be affected.

environmentalism: The belief that humans have an obligation to protect the world from the excesses of human habitation, including pollution and the destruction of wilderness.

equality of opportunity: When all people are given the same chances to compete and achieve so that those with talent and diligence will succeed, whereas others will not.

equality of outcome: When all people achieve the same result, regardless of talent or effort.

equal protection clause: Part of the Fourteenth Amendment, which states that states must give all citizens the equal protection of the law.

Equal Rights Amendment: A proposed amendment that would end gender discrimination; it failed to be ratified.

equal time rule: A broadcast media regulation that requires media outlets to give equal amounts of time to opposing candidates in an election.

equity: When all parties to a transaction are treated fairly.

establishment clause: A part of the First Amendment that forbids government establishment of religion.

excess demand: An economic situation in which the demand for something exceeds the supply.

exclusionary rule: A legal rule that excludes from trial evidence obtained in an illegal search.

executive leadership: The view that the president should have strong influence over the bureaucracy.

Executive Office of the President: A set of agencies that work closely with the president to help him perform his job.

executive order: An order issued by the president that has the effect of law.

executive privilege: The right of officials of the executive branch to refuse to disclose some information to other branches of government or to the public.

ex post facto law: A law that declares something illegal after it has been done.

expressed powers: The specific powers given to Congress or the president by the Constitution; also called the *enumerated powers.*

F

fairness doctrine: A broadcast media regulation that requires a broadcaster that airs a controversial program to also provide airtime to people with an opposing view.

faithless elector: An elector who votes for someone other than the candidate who won the most votes in the state.

fascism: Ideology from Italy that stresses national unity, a strong expansionist military, and absolute rule by one party.

federal budget: A document detailing how the federal government will spend money during a fiscal year.

Federal Communications Commission: The federal agency that regulates the broadcast media.

Federal Election Campaign Act: A law, passed in 1971, that limited expenditures on media advertising and required disclosure of donations above $100; made more stringent following the Watergate scandal.

Federal Election Commission: The independent agency established in 1974 to enforce campaign finance laws.

federalism: A system of government in which power is shared by national and state governments.

Federal Register: A federal publication that lists all executive orders.

federal reserve bank: The name of the central bank of the United States; often called the Fed.

federal system: A system of government where power is shared between the central government and state and local governments.

feminism: The belief that women are equal to men and should be treated equally by the law.

filibuster: A Senate tactic; a senator in the minority on a bill holds the floor (in effect shutting down the Senate) until the majority backs down and kills the bill.

First Continental Congress: A gathering of representatives from all thirteen colonies in 1774; it called for a total boycott of British goods in protest against taxes.

fiscal federalism: The practice of states spending federal money to help administer national programs.

fiscal policy: How the government influences the economy through taxing, borrowing, and spending.

fiscal year: A twelve-month period (which does not coincide with the calendar year) used for accounting and budget purposes by the federal government.

527 groups: A political organization, not affiliated with a party, that can raise and spend soft money; named after a section of the Internal Revenue Code.

flat taxes: A taxation system in which everyone is charged the same rate, regardless of income.

food stamps: Coupons issued by the government that can be used to purchase food.

foreign policy: A state's international goals and its strategies to achieve those goals.

formalized rules: Another term for standard operating procedure.

formula grants: Grants in which a formula is used to determine how much money each state receives.

framers: The men who wrote the Constitution.

franking: The ability of members of Congress to mail informational literature to constituents free of charge.

free exercise clause: The part of the First Amendment that forbids the government from interfering in the free exercise of religion.

free rider: A person who benefits from an interest group's efforts without actually contributing to those efforts.

front-loading: Moving primaries up in the campaign calendar so that many primaries are held early in the campaign.

front-runner: The candidate perceived to be in the lead in an election campaign.

full faith and credit clause: A clause in Article IV of the Constitution that declares that state governments must give full faith and credit to other state governments' decisions.

fundamentalism: The belief that a religious document is infallible and literally true.

G

gag order: An order by a court to block people from talking or writing about a trial.

gender discrimination: Treating people differently and unequally because of gender.

general election: An election contest between all party nominees and independent candidates; the winner becomes a member of Congress.

general jurisdiction: A court's power to hear cases, which is mostly unrestricted.

gerrymandering: The term used to describe the process by which the party that controls the state government uses redistricting to its own political advantage.

Gibbons v. Ogden: An 1824 Supreme Court case that gave the federal government extensive powers through the commerce clause.

Gideon v. Wainwright: Supreme Court case of 1963 that ordered governments to provide an attorney to criminal defendants who cannot afford one.

globalization: The trend toward the breakdown of state borders and the rise of international and global organizations and governments.

government: The organization of power within a country.

Government Accountability Office: Congress's main investigative agency, the GAO investigates operations of government agencies as part of congressional oversight.

government bond: A promissory note issued by the government to pay back the purchase price plus interest.

government corporation: A federal agency that operates like a corporation (following business practices and charging for services) but receives some federal funding.

grandfather clause: A voting law that stated that a person could vote if his grandfather was eligible to vote prior to 1867; designed to keep blacks from voting.

grant-in-aid: A general term to describe federal aid given to the states for a particular matter.

grant of power: Declaring that a certain person or group has a specific power.

grassroots activism: Efforts to influence the government by mobilizing large numbers of people.

Great Compromise: The compromise plan on representation in the constitutional convention; it created a bicameral legislature with representation determined by population in one house and equality in the other; also known as the *Connecticut Compromise.*

gross domestic product: The total value of all economic transactions within a state.

guerrilla war: A war in which one or both combatants use small, lightly armed militia units rather than professional, organized armies; guerrilla fighters usually seek to topple their government, often enjoying the support of the people.

gun control: Policies that aim at regulating and reducing the use of firearms.

H

Hatch Act: A law passed in 1939 that restricts the participation of federal civil servants in political campaigns.

hierarchy: An arrangement of power with a small number of people at the top issuing orders through a chain of command to lower-level workers; each person is responsible to someone above him or her.

home rule: The granting of significant autonomy to local governments by state governments.

home style: The way a member of Congress behaves in his or her district.

honeymoon period: The first few months of an administration in which the public, members of Congress, and the media tend to give the president their goodwill.

horizontal federalism: How state governments relate to one another.

hyperpluralism: The idea that there are too many interest groups competing for benefits.

I

idealism: The view that states should act in the global arena to promote moral causes and use ethical means to achieve them.

ideology: A set of beliefs a person holds that shape the way he or she behaves and sees the world.

GLOSSARY

illegal participation: Political activity that includes illegal actions, such as sabotage or assassination.

impeachment: The power of the House of Representatives to charge an officeholder with crimes; the Senate then holds a trial to determine if the officeholder should be expelled from office.

implementation: The act of putting laws into practice.

implied powers: Powers given to the national government by the necessary and proper clause.

income distribution: The way income is distributed among the population.

income transfer: A government action that takes money from one part of the citizenry and gives it to another part; usually the transfer goes from the well-off to the poor.

incorporation: The practice of federal courts forcing state governments to abide by the Bill of Rights.

incrementalism: The tendency of policy in the United States to change gradually, in small ways, rather than dramatically.

independent: A person who does not feel affiliation for any party.

independent executive agency: A federal agency that is not part of any department; its leader reports directly to the president.

independent regulatory agency: A federal agency charged with regulating some part of the economy; in theory, such agencies are independent of Congress and the president.

individualism: The idea that all people are different and should be able to make their own choices.

inflation: The increase of prices.

informational benefits: The educational benefits people derive from belonging to an interest group and learning more about the issues they care about.

inherent powers: The powers inherent to the national government because the United States is a sovereign nation.

in-kind subsidies: Government aid to poor people that is not given as cash but in forms such as food stamps and rent vouchers.

inside game: Interest groups' efforts to influence government by direct and close contact with government officials; also known as *lobbying*.

interest group: An organization of people who share a common interest and work together to protect and promote that interest by influencing the government.

international agreement: An understanding between states to restrict their behavior and set up rules governing international affairs.

internationalism: The view that the United States should play an active role in world affairs.

international law: A set of agreements, traditions, and norms built up over time that restricts what states can do; not always binding.

international organization: An institution set up by agreements between nations, such as the United Nations and the World Trade Organization.

international system: The basic structures that affect how states relate to one another, including rules and traditions.

Internet media: Media that is distributed online.

interpretive reporting: Reporting that states the facts along with analysis and interpretation.

intervention: When a state sends military forces to help a country that is already at war.

iron triangle: An alliance of groups with an interest in a policy area: bureaucrats from the relevant agency, legislators from appropriate committees, and interest groups affected by the issue.

isolationism: The view that the United States should largely ignore the rest of the world.

issue advertising: Advertising, paid for by outside groups, that can criticize or praise a candidate but not explicitly say "vote for X" or "vote against X."

issue network: A collection of actors who agree on a policy and work together to shape policy.

J

Jim Crow laws: Laws passed by southern states that imposed inequality and segregation on blacks.

Joint Chiefs of Staff: A group that helps the president make strategy decisions and evaluates the needs and capabilities of the military.

judicial activism: A judicial philosophy that argues courts must take an active positive role to remedy wrongs in the country.

judicial implementation: The process of enforcing a court's ruling.

judicial philosophy: A set of ideas that shape how a judge or lawyer interprets the law and the Constitution.

judicial restraint: A judicial philosophy that believes the court's responsibility is to interpret the law, not set policy.

judicial review: The power of the courts to declare laws and presidential actions unconstitutional.

jurisdiction: A court's power to hear cases of a particular type.

justiciable question: A matter that the courts can review.

just-war theory: A theory of ethics that defines when war is morally permissible and what means of warfare are justified.

K

Keynesian economics: A demand-side economic policy, first presented by John Maynard Keynes after World War I, that encouraged deficit spending by governments during economic recessions in order to provide jobs and boost income.

kitchen cabinet: An informal name for the president's closest advisers.

Kyoto Protocol: An international treaty aimed at reducing greenhouse gas emissions.

L

laissez-faire capitalism: The economic philosophy that the government should not interfere with the economy.

lawmaking: The power to make rules that are binding on all people in a society.

layer-cake federalism: A term used to describe federalism through most of the nineteenth century, in which the federal and state governments each had their own issue areas, that rarely overlapped; also known as *dual federalism*.

legislative agenda: A series of laws a person wishes to pass.

legitimacy: Acceptance by citizens of the government.

Lemon test: A three-part test to determine if the establishment clause has been violated; named for the 1971 case *Lemon v. Kurtzman.*

libel: Printing false statements that defame a person's character.

liberalism: A theory of international relations that deemphasizes the importance of military power in favor of economic power, trade, and international institutions.

libertarianism: The belief that government should be small and most decisions left up to the individual.

liberty: The freedom to do what one chooses as long as one does not harm or limit the freedom of other people.

limited government: A government that places few restrictions on its citizens' choices and actions, and in which the government is limited in what it can do.

limited jurisdiction: A court's power to hear only certain kinds of cases.

limited war: A war fought primarily between professional armies to achieve specific political objectives without causing widespread destruction.

line-item veto: A special type of veto that the president can use to strike the specific parts of the bill he or she dislikes without rejecting the entire bill.

line organization: In the government bureaucracy, an agency whose head reports directly to the president.

literacy test: Historically, a test that must be passed before a person can vote; designed to prevent blacks from voting.

lobbying: Attempting to persuade government officials through direct contact via persuasion and the provision of material benefits; also known as the *inside game.*

logrolling: A practice in Congress where two or more members agree to support each other's bills.

loophole: A part of a tax code that allows individuals or businesses to reduce their tax burden.

loose constructionism: A judicial philosophy that believes the Constitution should be interpreted in an open way, not limited to things explicitly stated.

M

machine: A very strong party organization that turns favors and patronage into votes.

Madisonian Model: A structure of government proposed by James Madison that avoided tyranny by separating power among different branches and building checks and balances into the Constitution.

majority leader: (1) In the House, the second-ranking member of the majority party; (2) in the Senate, the highest-ranking member of the majority party.

majority opinion: A court opinion that reflects the reasoning of the majority of justices.

majority party: In a legislative body, the party with more than half of the seats.

majority rule: The idea that the government should act in accordance with the will of the majority of people.

malapportionment: An apportionment of seats in Congress that is unfair due to population shifts.

mandate: When the federal government requires states to do certain things.

mandatory retirement: An employment policy that states that when an employee reaches a certain age, he or she must retire.

marble-cake federalism: A term used to describe federalism for most of the twentieth century (and into the twenty-first), where the federal government and the states work closely together and are intertwined; also known as *cooperative federalism.*

markup: When a Congressional committee revises a bill in session.

material incentive: The lure of a concrete benefit, usually money, that attracts people to join a group.

McCain-Feingold bill: The popular informal name for the Bipartisan Campaign Finance Reform Act of 2002; it is named after its sponsors, Republican John McCain and Democrat Russell Feingold.

McCulloch v. Maryland: A Supreme Court case that granted the federal government extensive power to carry out its enumerated powers.

means-testing: Basing benefits from a policy on a person's wealth so that poor people get more benefits than rich people.

media: Information and the organizations that distribute that information to the public.

media consolidation: The trend toward a few large corporations owning most of the media outlets in the country.

merit system: The practice of hiring and promoting people based on skill.

Merit System Protection Board: A board that investigates charges of wrongdoing in the federal civil service.

midterm election: A congressional election that does not coincide with a presidential election.

military aid: Assistance to other countries designed to strengthen the recipient's military.

military-industrial complex: The alliance of defense contractors, the military, and some members of Congress that promotes a large defense budget in order to profit themselves.

minority leader: In both the House and Senate, the leader of the minority party.

minority party: In a legislative body, the party with fewer than half of the seats.

Miranda v. Arizona: A 1966 case in which the Supreme Court ruled that police must inform suspects of their rights when arrested.

mixed economy: An economy that includes elements of the free market and central planning.

monarchy: A regime in which all power is held by a single person.

monetary policy: An economic policy that seeks to control the supply of money in the economy.

monopolistic model: A view of the bureaucracy that says bureaucracies have no incentive to reform or improve performance because they face no competition.

Monroe Doctrine: An American policy, set by President James Monroe in 1823, that claims America's right to intervene in the affairs of Western Hemisphere nations.

multiculturalism: The idea that Americans should learn about and respect the many cultural heritages of the people of the United States.

multilateralism: The idea that nations should act together to solve problems.

multinational corporation: A business that operates in more than one country.

multiple-member district: A legislative district that sends more than one person to the legislature.

multipolar system: An international system with more than two major powers.

N

nation: A large group of people who are linked by a similar culture, language, and history.

national convention: A convention held by a political party every four years to nominate candidates for president and vice president and to ratify the party platform.

national debt: Money owed by a government.

national interest: Things that will benefit and protect a state.

nationalism: A belief in the goodness of one's nation and a desire to help make the nation stronger and better.

National Security Council: A part of the White House Staff that advises the president on security policy.

nation-building: The task of creating a national identity through promotion of common culture, language, and history.

nation-state: A state that rules over a single nation.

Nazism: Political ideology from Germany that stressed the superiority of the German race, authoritarian rule by one party, military expansion, and a longing for a mythical past.

necessary and proper clause: A clause at the end of Article I, Section 8, of the U.S. Constitution that grants Congress the power to do whatever is necessary and proper to carry out its duties; also known as the *elastic clause.*

necessary evil: Something that is believed to be needed but is not good in and of itself; many Americans see government as a necessary evil.

negotiated rule-making: A federal rule-making process that includes those affected by the rules.

neoconservatism: A recent development in American conservatism that believes the power of the state should be used to promote conservative goals.

New Deal coalition: The supporters of Franklin Roosevelt's New Deal; the coalition included labor unions, Catholics, southern whites, and African Americans; helped the Democrats dominate politics from the 1930s until the 1960s.

new federalism: An American movement, starting in the 1970s, to return power to state and local governments, thereby decreasing the amount of power held by the federal government.

New Jersey Plan: A plan at the constitutional convention that gave each state equal representation in the legislature.

nihilism: The belief that in order to remake society, one must first destroy the current society.

Nineteenth Amendment: Passed in 1920, it gave women the right to vote.

No Child Left Behind Act: A law passed in 2001 that expanded federal funding to schools but required increased testing and accountability.

noneconomic group: An interest group that works on noneconomic issues; also called a *citizens' group.*

nongovernmental actor: A participant in the international arena that is not part of a government; such participants include nongovernmental organizations, multinational corporations, and international organizations.

nongovernmental organization: A political actor that is not affiliated with a particular government. Many NGOs are nonprofit institutions run by private citizens, such as the Red Cross, Doctors Without Borders, and the Catholic Church.

Nuclear Non-Proliferation Treaty: An international treaty, signed in 1968, that aims to prevent the spread of nuclear weapons.

0

objective reporting: Reporting only the facts with no opinion or bias.

office-block ballot: A ballot that groups candidates by office: All candidates for an office are listed together; also called the *Massachusetts ballot.*

Office of Personnel Management: The central federal personnel office, created in 1978.

oligarchy: Rule by the wealthy few.

ombudsperson: A person who investigates complaints against government agencies or employees.

open primary: A primary in which a person can participate in any party's primary as long as he or she participates in only one party's primary.

open rule: A rule on a bill, issued by the House Rules Committee, allowing amendments during floor debate.

opinion: A document issued by a court explaining the reasons for its decision.

opinion leader: A person whose opinion can shape the opinions of many others.

original intent: A judicial philosophy that states that judges should seek to interpret the law and the constitution in line with the intent of the founders.

original jurisdiction: The authority to be the first court to hear a case.

outside game: A term used to describe grassroots activism and other means to influence elections and policymaking.

overregulation: An excess of regulation that hurts efficiency.

oversight: Congress's power to make sure laws are being properly enforced.

P

pack journalism: The idea that journalists frequently copy and imitate each other rather than doing independent reporting.

paradox of participation: When many people vote because they wish to make a difference, but the actual chances of making a difference are infinitesimally small.

pardon: A release from punishment for criminal conviction; the president has the power to pardon.

parliamentary democracy: A regime in which the legislature chooses the executive branch.

partisan journalism: Journalism that advances the viewpoint of a political party.

party activist: A person who is deeply involved with a party; usually more ideologically extreme than an average party voter.

party-centered politics: Campaigns and politics that focus on party labels and platforms.

party-column ballot: A ballot that groups candidates by party; also called the *Indiana ballot.*

party identification: Feeling connected to a political party.

party in government: The role and function of parties in government, particularly in Congress.

party in the electorate: Party identification among voters.

party organization: The formal structure and leadership of a political party.

party platform: The collection of issue positions endorsed by a political party.

party reform: Measures aimed at opening up party leadership adopted by the major parties following the 1968 election.

patronage: Government jobs and contracts given out to political allies in exchange for support.

Pendleton Act: Another name for the Civil Service Reform Act of 1883.

per curiam: An unsigned decision issued by an appellate court; it reaffirms the lower court's ruling.

pigeonholing: The ability of a committee to kill a bill by setting it aside and not acting on it.

Plessy v. Ferguson: The Supreme Court case of 1896 that upheld a Louisiana law segregating passengers on trains; it created the separate but equal doctrine.

pluralism: The view that society contains numerous centers of power and many people participate in making decisions for society.

plurality: More votes than any other candidate but not a majority.

plurality opinion: An opinion written by the majority of justices on the winning side.

pocket veto: An unusual type of presidential veto: When the president neither signs nor vetoes a bill, after ten days the bill dies if Congress is not in session.

political action committee: An organization, usually allied with an interest group, that can donate money to political campaigns.

political appointees: Federal bureaucrats appointed by the president, often to reward loyalty.

political culture: The set of beliefs, values, shared myths, and notions of a good polity that a group of people hold.

political economy: The study of how politics and economics interact.

political efficacy: The belief that the government listens to normal people and that participation can make a difference in government.

political equality: Treating everyone the same way in the realm of politics.

political participation: Engaging in actions to achieve political goals.

political party: An alliance of like-minded people who work together to win elections and control of the government.

political science: The systematic, rigorous study of politics.

political socialization: The process by which political culture is passed on to the young.

politics: The process by which government decisions are made.

polling: Assessing public opinion by asking people what they think and feel.

pollster: A person who conducts polls.

poll tax: A fee for voting, designed to keep blacks and other poor people from voting.

popular sovereignty: A regime in which the government must respond to the wishes of the people.

Populists: A political movement in the late nineteenth century that fought on behalf of the poor workers and farmers; fused with the Democratic Party in 1896.

pork: Money spent by Congress for local projects that are not strictly necessary and are designed to funnel money into a district.

poverty line: The federal standard for poverty: Anyone below a certain income level is considered poor.

power: The ability to get others to do what you want.

power of the purse: The ability of Congress to spend money; all federal expenditures must be authorized by Congress.

precedent: A court ruling bearing on subsequent court cases.

preemption: The practice of the national government overriding state and local laws in the name of the national interest.

Presidential Commission: A body that advises the president on some problem, making recommendations; some are temporary, whereas others are permanent.

presidential democracy: A regime in which the president and the legislators must be entirely separate.

president pro tempore: In the vice president's absence, the presiding officer of the Senate.

primary election: An election within a party to choose the party's nominee for the office.

print media: Media distributed via printed materials.

prior restraint: Stopping free expression before it happens.

private bill: A bill that offers benefit or relief to a single person, named in the bill.

private good: A good that benefits only some people, such as members of a group.

privatization: The practice of private companies providing government services.

privileges and immunities clause: Part of the Fourteenth Amendment, which forbids state governments from taking away any of the privileges and immunities of American citizenship.

probability sample: A sampling technique in which each member of the population has a known chance of being chosen for the sample.

professional legislature: A state legislature that meets in session for long periods, pays its members well, and hires large support staffs for legislators.

progressive taxes: A taxation system in which the rich must pay a higher percentage of their income than the poor.

prohibited powers: The powers specifically denied to the national government by the Constitution.

project grants: Categorical grant programs in which states submit proposals for projects to the federal government and the national government chooses which to fund on a competitive basis.

proportional representation: An electoral system in which each party gets a number of seats in the legislature proportionate to its percentage of the vote.

prospective voting: Making a vote choice by looking to the future: Voters choose the candidate(s) they believe will help the country the most in the next few years.

proxy war: A war fought by third parties rather than by the enemy states themselves.

public administration: The task of running the government, and providing services through policy implementation.

public assistance: Another term for *welfare.*

public education: Informing the public about key issues and about what Congress is doing about those issues.

public good: A good that benefits everyone, not just some; also called *collective good.*

public opinion: The basic attitudes and opinions of the general public.

public policy: Any rule, plan, or action pertaining to issues of domestic national importance.

public representative role: The role of the media to act as a representative of the public, holding government officials accountable to the people.

purposive incentive: The lure of a desire to promote a cause.

R

rally 'round the flag effect: A significant boost in presidential popularity when a foreign crisis arises.

random selection: A sampling technique to ensure that each person in the population has an equal chance of being selected for the sample.

ranking member: The senior committee member from the minority party.

ratings game: The practice of organizations rating members of Congress based on votes that matter to the organizations and their members.

rational choice theory: An approach that assumes people act rationally in their self-interest, seeking to maximize value.

rationalism: The belief that human reason can find solutions to many of our problems.

realignment: A dramatic shift in the balance of the two parties that changes the key issues dividing the parties.

realism: A theory of international relations that stresses the importance of power (particularly military power) and claims that states act in their national interest.

reapportionment: The process of reallocating representation in the House of Representatives after a census; some states will gain seats, while other will lose them.

recession: An economic downturn; milder than a depression.

redistributive policy: A government action that takes money from one part of the citizenry and gives it to another part; usually the transfer goes from the well-off to the poor; also known as *income transfer.*

redistricting: Redrawing district boundaries after a state loses or gains seats in the House of Representatives.

regime: A word used to describe a particular government.

regressive taxes: A taxation system that costs the poor a larger portion of their income than it does the rich because the amount of tax gets smaller as the amount to which the tax is applied gets larger.

regulated federalism: The practice of the national government imposing standards and regulations on state governments.

regulatory policy: Government policies that limit what businesses can do; examples include minimum wages, workplace safety measures, and careful monitoring of stock sales.

remand: Sending a case back to a lower court for a new trial or proceeding.

rent voucher: A voucher issued by the government that can be used to pay all or part of a poor person's rent.

representative democracy: A system of government in which the people elect officials to represent their interests in the government.

representative sample: A sample that resembles the population as a whole.

reprieve: A formal postponement of the execution of a criminal sentence; the president has the power to grant reprieves.

republic: A regime that runs by representative democracy.

reregulation: Significantly changing government regulations on an industry.

reserved powers: The powers reserved to the states and the people in the Tenth Amendment.

responsible party: A party that is strong enough to carry out a specific platform if elected to office.

retention election: A state election, held in states using the merit plan for selecting judges, in which voters are asked whether a judge should keep his or her job.

retrospective voting: Making a vote choice by looking to the past: Voters support incumbents if they feel that the country has done well over the past few years.

revenue agency: A government agency that raises money by collecting taxes or fees.

revenue sharing: The practice of the federal government giving money to the states with no strings attached; started by the Nixon Administration and ended by the Reagan Administration.

reverse: When a court overturns a lower court's ruling, declaring it void.

reverse discrimination: Discrimination against majority-status people due to affirmative action policies.

revolution: A major event causing a fundamental change in a state.

rider: An amendment attached to a bill that has nothing to do with the bill itself.

right of rebuttal: A media regulation that requires broadcasters to give people an opportunity to reply to criticisms aired on the outlet.

rights of the minority: Rights held by the minority that must be respected by the majority.

Roe v. Wade: A 1973 Supreme Court case that legalized abortion during the first trimester.

rogue state: A state that does not follow international law or unspoken rules of the global arena.

roll-call vote: Occurs when each member's vote is recorded.

rugged individualism: A form of individualism that emphasizes self-reliance and ignoring what others want and think.

rule-making: The bureaucratic function of creating rules needed to implement policy.

rule of four: An informal rule in the Supreme Court: Four justices must agree to hear a case for the Court to issue a writ of certiorari.

S

sample: A group of people who are used to stand in for the whole population in a poll.

sampling error: Mistakes in polls caused by bad samples.

school vouchers: Government money given to parents to help pay for tuition at private schools.

Second Continental Congress: The governing body over the colonies during the revolution that drafted the Articles of Confederation to create the first national government.

selective incentives: The lure of benefits that only group members will receive.

selective incorporation: Forcing states to abide by only parts of the Bill of Rights, not the whole thing.

self-selected candidate: A person who chooses to run for office on his or her own initiative.

senatorial courtesy: A tradition in which a Senator, if he or she is of the president's party, gets input into nominees for federal judgeships in his or her state.

separation of powers: Dividing up governmental power among several branches.

sexual harassment: Unwanted and inappropriate physical or verbal conduct of a sexual nature that interferes with doing one's job or creates a hostile work environment.

Shays' Rebellion: A 1786 uprising of Massachusetts farmers against high taxes and debt.

signing message: A message attached to a bill the president signs, explaining his or her understanding of the bill.

single-member district: A legislative district that sends only one person to the legislature.

skewed sample: A sample that is not representative and leads to inaccurate polling results; a deceptive practice used to manipulate public opinion.

slander: Publicly stating things that the speaker knows to be untrue that hurt a person's reputation.

social capital: Mutual trust and habits of cooperation that are acquired by people through involvement in community organizations and volunteer groups.

socialism: Political view that the free market breeds servitude and inequality and should be abolished.

social security: A social insurance program that aims to keep retired people and the disabled out of poverty.

sociological representation: A type of representation in which the representative resembles the constituents in ethnic, religious, racial, social, or educational ways.

soft money: Unregulated money raised by parties and spent to influence elections indirectly; banned by the 2002 Bipartisan Campaign Reform Act.

solicitor general: A high-ranking Justice Department official who submits requests for writs of certiorari to the Supreme Court on behalf of the federal government; he or she also usually argues cases for the government in front the Court.

solidarity incentive: The lure of a social benefit, such as friendship, gained by members of an organization.

sovereignty: The right to exercise political power in a territory.

Speaker of the House: The leader of the House of Representatives, elected by the majority party.

special district: A type of local government designed to meet a very specific need.

special election: An election to replace a member of Congress who leaves office in between regular elections.

specialization: The practice of a group or person becoming extremely knowledgeable and skilled at one specific task.

splinter party: A third party formed when a faction from a major party breaks off and forms its own party.

split-ticket voting: Voting for candidates from one party for some offices and from the other party for other offices.

spoiler: A losing candidate who costs another candidate the election.

spoils system: The practice of an elected officials rewarding supporters and allies by giving them government jobs.

staffer: A person who works for Congress in a supporting capacity.

standard operating procedure: A set of rules established in a bureaucracy that dictate how workers respond to different situations so that all workers respond in the same way.

stare decisis: The legal doctrine of following precedent.

state: A political unit that has sovereign power over a particular piece of land.

statecraft: The exercise of power, guided by wisdom, in pursuit of the public good.

State of the Union address: A constitutionally mandated message, given by the president to Congress, in which the president lays out plans for the coming year.

statute: A law passed by Congress, a state legislature, or some other government body.

stewardship theory: A view of presidential power, put forward by Theodore Roosevelt, arguing that the president is uniquely suited to act for the well-being of the whole nation because he or she is elected by the whole nation.

straight-ticket voting: Voting for only candidates from one party.

strict constructionism: A judicial philosophy that argues that constitutional interpretation should be limited to the specific wording of the document.

subnationalism: Identification with small ethnic and regional groups within a nation.

suffrage: The right to vote; also called the *franchise.*

sunset provisions: Expiration dates written into some federal programs; Congress can renew the program if it is satisfied that the program is achieving its objectives.

sunshine laws: Laws that require government agencies to hold public proceedings on a regular basis.

superdelegate: A party leader or elected official who is automatically granted delegate status for the national convention; superdelegates do not have to be chosen in primaries.

Super Tuesday: A term used to describe primary elections held in a large number of states on the same day.

Supplemental Security Income: A federal program that provides a minimum income to seniors and the disabled who do not qualify for social security.

supply-side economics: An attempt to improve the economy by providing big tax cuts to businesses and wealthy individuals (the supply side). These cuts encourage investment, which then creates jobs, so the effect will be felt throughout the economy; also known as *trickle-down economics.*

supremacy clause: The part of Article VI of the Constitution that specifies that the federal Constitution, and laws passed by the federal government, are the supreme law of the land.

supremacy doctrine: The doctrine that national law takes priority over state law; included in the Constitution as the supremacy clause.

surplus: When a government spends less money than it takes in.

symbolic speech: Actions that are intended to convey a belief.

system of government: How power is distributed among different parts and levels of the state.

T

talk radio: A radio format featuring a host who interviews guests that is often very partisan.

tax credit: A reduction in one's tax burden designed to help certain people.

Temporary Assistance to Need Families: A federal welfare program that provides money to poor families.

term limits: Limits on the number of terms an elected official can serve.

terrorism: The use of violent tactics with the aim of creating fear and destabilizing a government; frequently targets civilians.

third party: In American politics, any political party other than the Democrats and Republicans.

Three-Fifths Compromise: A compromise on how to count slaves for determining population; slaves were counted as three-fifths of a person.

totalitarian government: A regime in which the government controls every facet of life.

total war: A highly destructive total war in which combatants use every resource available to destroy the social fabric of the enemy.

transnational: Something that lies beyond the boundaries of a nation-state or consists of several nation-states.

trickle-down economics: An attempt to improve the economy by providing big tax cuts to businesses and wealthy individuals (the supply side). These cuts encourage investment, which then creates jobs, so the effect will be felt throughout the economy; also known as *supply-side economics*.

trustee representation: A type of representation in which the people choose a representative whose judgment and experience they trust. The representative votes for what he or she thinks is right, regardless of the opinions of the constituents.

tyranny of the majority: When the majority violate the rights of the minority.

U

unconventional participation: Political activity that, although legal, is not considered appropriate by many people; it includes demonstrations, boycotts, and protests.

underemployment: When people who seek work can only find part-time jobs.

unemployment: When not everyone who wants a job can find one.

unfunded mandate: A mandate for which the federal government gives the states no money.

unilateral: A state acting alone in the global arena.

unipolar: An international system with a single superpower dominating other states.

unitary system: A system of government where power is concentrated in the hands of the central government.

unity: The idea that people overwhelmingly support the government and share certain common beliefs even if they disagree about particular policies.

user fee: A fee charged by the government to do certain things (e.g., paying a toll to use a tunnel).

V

veto: The power of the president to stop a bill passed by Congress from becoming law.

veto message: A message written by the president, attached to a bill he or she has vetoed, which explains the reasons for the veto.

Virginia Plan: A plan at the constitutional convention to base representation in the legislature on population.

voter turnout: The percentage of citizens who vote in an election.

voting behavior: A term used to describe the motives and factors that shape voters' choices.

Voting Rights Act: A law passed in 1965 that banned discrimination in voter registration requirements.

W

War Powers Resolution: Passed by Congress in 1973, the War Powers Resolution demands that the president consult with Congress when sending troops into action; it also gives Congress the power to force withdrawal of troops.

Washington community: The "inside the beltway" group that closely follows politics and constantly evaluates the relative power of politicians.

watchdog journalism: Journalism that attempts to hold government officials and institutions accountable for their actions.

Weberian model: The model of bureaucracy developed by sociologist Max Weber that characterizes bureaucracy as a rational and efficient means of organizing a large group of people.

welfare: The term for the set of policies designed to help those in economic need.

welfare state: The term to describe the government or country that provides aid to the poor and help to the unemployed.

whip: A member of the leadership of a legislative body responsible for counting votes and connecting the leadership with the rank and file.

whistleblower: A person who reports wrongdoing in a government agency.

White House staff: The people with whom the president works every day.

white primary: The practice of political parties only allowing whites to participate in their primaries.

winner take all: An electoral system in which the person with the most votes wins everything (and everyone else loses); most states have winner-take-all systems for determining electoral votes.

writ of certiorari: The legal document, issued by the Supreme Court, that orders a lower court to send a case to the Supreme Court for review.

writ of habeas corpus: A court order requiring that the government show cause for detaining someone and charge him or her with a crime.

Y

yellow journalism: Journalism that focuses on shocking and sordid stories to sell newspapers.

GLOSSARY

Index